Catherine Atkinson has a degree is). She has been Deputy Cookery Edine and later Cookery Editor of *Home.* (er and food consultant to various lifes as written more than sixty cookbooks. She specialises in healthy eating and her recent published books include *Coconut Water and Coconut Oil*, *Nut Milks and Nut Butters* and *Power Blends and Smoothies.*

Other titles

Power Blend and Smoothies

How To Make Your Own Cordials and Syrups

How To Make Perfect Panini

Brilliant Breadmaking in Your Bread Machine

The High Speed Blender Cookbook

Everyday Family Recipes for Your Combination Microwave

Everyday Lebanese Cooking

A Lebanese Feast

Pâtisserie

Southern Italian Family Cooking

Traditional Country Preserving

Afternoon Tea

Everyday Thai Cooking

Everyday Curries

Everyday Healthy Indian Cookery

The Healthy Slow Cooker Cookbook

Fermenting Food for Healthy Eating

Catherine Atkinson

A How To Book

ROBINSON

First published in Great Britain in 2018 by Robinson

Copyright © Catherine Atkinson, 2018

10 9 8 7 6 5 4 3 2 1

The moral right of the author has been asserted.

All rights reserved.
No part of this publication may be reproduced, stored in a retrieval system, or transmitted, in any form, or by any means, without the prior permission in writing of the publisher, nor be otherwise circulated in any form of binding or cover other than that in which it is published and without a similar condition including this condition being imposed on the subsequent purchaser.

A CIP catalogue record for this book is available from the British Library.

ISBN: 978-1-4721-4051-7

Typeset by Basement Press, Glaisdale
Printed and bound in Great Britain by Clays Ltd, St Ives plc

Papers used by Robinson are from well-managed forests and other sustainable sources.

Robinson
An imprint of
Little, Brown Book Group
Carmelite House
50 Victoria Embankment
London EC4Y 0DZ

An Hachette UK Company
www.hachette.co.uk

www.littlebrown.co.uk

How To Books are published by Robinson, an imprint of Little, Brown Book Group. We welcome proposals from authors who have first-hand experience of their subjects. Please set out the aims of your book, its target market and its suggested contents in an email to Nikki.Read@howtobooks.co.uk

Contents

1 AN INTRODUCTION TO FERMENTATION AND ITS BENEFITS 1
Why we need microbes and enzymes 1
What is fermentation? 3
How fermented food support good health 3
Eating fermented foods to prevent illness 4
Choose your ingredients 8
Equipment 12
Sterilising equipment 15
Simple steps for safe fermenting 17
Getting started 18

2 FERMENTING VEGETABLES AND FRUIT 19
Top tips for fermenting vegetables and fruit 19
Using a starter culture 20
Seasonings, spices and flavours 21
Simple sauerkraut, step by step 23
Spiced red cabbage and apple sauerkraut 25
Mixed vegetable slaw 26
Dill pickles 28
Fermented spring vegetables 30
Cauliflower, carrot and pepper pickles 31
Pickled radishes with red onion and apple 32
Classic kimchi 34
Chunky kimchi 36
White kimchi 38
Pickled beetroot and turnips 40
Carrot kraut with ginger and orange 41
Preserved lemons 42
Probiotic tomato ketchup 43
Pineapple pickle 44
Fermented mango preserve 45

3 FERMENTED DAIRY AND DAIRY ALTERNATIVES 47

Yogurt **49**
Greek yogurt and whey **50**
Labneh **51**
Coconut yogurt **52**
Coconut drinking yogurt **54**
Soured cream **56**
Cultured butter and buttermilk **57**
Milk kefir grains versus powdered kefir starter cultures 59
Tips for making kefir from milk kefir grains 60
Milk kefir **62**
Coconut milk kefir **64**
Kefir soft cheese **66**
Kefir cream **67**

4 FERMENTED DRINKS 69

Water kefir **70**
Coconut water kefir **72**
Kombucha **73**
Tips and troubleshooting when making kombucha 75
Rejuvelac **77**
Beetroot kvass **79**
Sparkling orange juice **80**
Probiotic limeade **81**

5 FERMENTED BREADS 83

Sourdough loaf **84**
Easy sourdough starter **87**
California sourdough **88**
Italian ciabatta **90**
Landbrot **92**

6 COOKING WITH FERMENTED FOODS 95

Soups, Starters and Snacks
Noodles in chilled beef broth **96**

Chicken miso soup **99**
Minted pea and broad bean soup with yogurt **101**
Borscht **102**
Thai-style vegetable omelette **103**
Griddled asparagus with yogurt hollandaise **104**
Easy mezze 105
  Tzatziki **105**
  Smoked aubergine and yogurt dip **106**
  Creamy hummus **107**
  Yogurt-spiced chicken skewers **108**
  Kefir ranch-style dip **109**
Marinated herring and beetroot salad **110**
Smoked salmon and pasta salad
  with avocado kefir dressing **111**
Summer chicken Caesar salad **112**
Salmon and kimchi sushi rolls **114**
Fresh tomato and kefir cheese bruschetta **116**
Couscous and grilled pepper salad with labneh **118**
Sesame chicken salad **120**
Quinoa falafels in wholemeal pittas
  with mixed vegetable slaw **122**
Creamy seafood wraps with kimchi **125**

Main Meals
Mango-stuffed chicken breasts **126**
Hunter's stew **128**
Paprika pork **130**
Mediterranean lamb kebabs **132**
Lamb tagine **133**
Miso-glazed halibut steaks **134**
Tempeh coconut korma **136**
Tempeh veggie-burgers **138**
Japanese red rice with natto **139**

Desserts
Sourdough pancakes **141**
Buttermilk panna cotta **142**
Berry frozen yogurt **143**

Fresh fruit jelly **144**
Coconut kefir cheesecake **146**
Chocolate and avocado mousse **148**
Tropical fruit salad **149**

Bakes and Cakes
Simple soda bread **150**
Brown buttermilk scones **152**
Creamy kefir carrot cake **154**
Yogurt cake with lemon and pistachios **156**

Six Super Smoothies
Breakfast blend **157**
Mango and orange wake-up **158**
Blueberry brain booster **159**
Pistachio and almond lassi **160**
Summer fruit sipper **161**
Avocado, coconut and pear smoothie **162**

INDEX 163

CHAPTER 1

An Introduction to Fermentation and its Benefits

While it may be considered the latest trend, fermentation as a way of preserving food dates back thousands of years and across the globe. Most countries have fermented foods in their culinary heritage, from sauerkraut in Germany to kimchi in Korea. People have fermented foods not just as a way to preserve them, but also for their nutritional and therapeutic value. The earliest records show evidence of this as far back as 6000 BC, and links between fermented food and health benefits were well documented in Ancient Rome.

Much later, in the nineteenth century, the research of Nobel Prize-winning microbiologist, Dr Élie Metchnikoff showed that beneficial bacteria could improve immunity; he also believed they helped slow down ageing. He named the yogurt-making bacteria *Lactobacillus bulgaricus* after the long-lived Bulgarian country people he studied. While his claims of longevity have never been proven, there is an increasing amount of evidence to indicate that gut bacteria play a vital role in immunity and that fermented food contributes to a healthy diet.

WHY WE NEED MICROBES AND ENZYMES

Many living things are so tiny they can only be seen through a microscope: they're known as microbes and come in three main types: bacteria, fungi (these include yeasts and moulds) and viruses.

For decades we have been obsessed with 'germs' (a word many people use for microbes), and most households have an army of products designed to destroy them, from bleach and disinfectant to cleaning sprays and detergents. The word 'anti-bacterial' increases product sales and appears on more and more items. Much of this is due to concerns about bacterial infections such as salmonella, listeria, botulism and MRSA, which have received so much attention in the press, we have almost forgotten that not all bacteria are bad. Despite our wide use of anti-bacterial products, there are still trillions of bacteria that live on and in our bodies; they are all over our skin and in our mouths, but the vast majority are in our guts and are known as gut microbiota (formerly gut flora). Most of these bacteria are 'good' bacteria, which keep harmful bacteria under control and help us fight infections. The last thing we want to do is destroy them, as they are hugely beneficial to our health. As well as enabling us to digest food, they manufacture B vitamins and chemicals such as serotonin, and can affect everything from our immunity to our moods, and even encourage weight loss. Although research is still in its early days, we now know that it is vital to maintain a good balance of gut bacteria to achieve optimal health.

With advances in technology and food production, an increasing choice of foods is available, yet most of us eat a more limited range than our ancestors. Many modern diets are low in nutrients and fibre and instead are packed with processed foods, refined carbohydrates and sugar. While these need not be harmful if eaten occasionally and in moderation, in an otherwise healthy and varied diet, a constantly poor diet of refined food will take its toll on health and may allow undesirable bacteria to thrive. The main function of the digestive system is to break down food so that nutrients can be absorbed by the body. When the intestines contain a balance of good and bad bacteria needed for good health, they are described as being in a state of symbiosis. When this process is disrupted it is known as 'dysbiosis', an imbalance in the gut microbiota caused by too few beneficial bacteria and an overgrowth of bad bacteria and yeasts. It's not junk food alone that causes imbalance: intensively reared meat, farmed fish and non-organic fruit and vegetables often contain small residues of antibiotics and pesticides that can interfere with gut bacteria. And if you are unwell and need a course of antibiotics, most of the beneficial gut bacteria may be wiped out, leaving you with a weak immune system and more prone to future illness.

However, it's not all doom and gloom. By making a few simple changes to your diet and including fermented foods, you can start to boost the diversity and number of beneficial gut bacteria in just a few days.

WHAT IS FERMENTATION?

There are many ways to preserve food. Most methods work by either destroying microbes or by preventing them from multiplying by depriving them of warmth or moisture or other conditions they need in order to thrive. Freezing, canning, drying, packing in salt, sugar, alcohol or vinegar are some of the ways we can preserve, i.e. prolong the keeping qualities of food.

Fermentation is one of the earliest and most traditional ways of preserving and the only one that actually increases a food's nutritional value. It works by preventing undesirable microbes from multiplying, by increasing the number of beneficial microbes: these are called probiotics, a word which literally means 'for life'. During fermentation, micro-organisms (bacteria and some beneficial yeasts) convert the sugar and starch in food into lactic acid in a process known as lacto-fermentation (carbon dioxide gas is a by-product of fermentation). It is the lactic acid that gives fermented foods and drinks their distinctive, slightly sour flavours.

HOW FERMENTED FOODS SUPPORT GOOD HEALTH

Many methods of preservation have a negative impact on the nutritional value of the food. At best they retain most of the nutrients of fresh food; at worst they may contain artificial chemicals or additives such as sugar that are detrimental to health. Fermentation is the only preservation method that actually improves the nutritional content of food as well as having numerous other health benefits.

- **Makes food more digestible** The bacteria that live in our gut are essential: they help with the digestion, absorption and assimilation of nutrients, so it's important to maintain a good balance of bacteria. Fermented food is easier to digest than non-fermented, as some of the sugars and starches in food are broken down during fermentation. In fermented drinks such as yogurt and kefir, most of the lactose is converted to simpler sugars, glucose and galactose, which break down further into lactic acid. Those who are only mildly lactose-intolerant are usually able to enjoy these foods.

- **Eliminates anti-nutrients** Compounds that interfere with the absorption of nutrients are known as anti-nutrients and these are destroyed by fermentation. Phytic acid, for example, is found in many legumes and grains and some vegetables; it reduces the absorption of valuable vitamins and minerals such as niacin, calcium, iron and zinc. Fermenting food (or sprouting, as in Rejuvelac, page 77) will neutralise much of the phytic acid. Miso and tempeh are examples of fermented legumes.
- **Increases vitamins and minerals** Fermentation increases the availability of many vitamins and minerals, particularly the B-group vitamins, as well as vitamins C, A and K.
- **Strengthens immunity** Fermented food and drinks repopulate your gut with friendly bacteria and restore balance in the gut, where a large proportion of the immune system is housed. These beneficial bacteria crowd out pathogenic bacteria and yeasts such as candida and provide health-supporting probiotics to make your immune system more robust. They also support the mucosa (gut lining) as a natural barrier, strengthening immunity.
- **Improves mood** The brain and gut are linked through the hypothalamic-pituitary-adrenal (HPA) axis and the gut is lined with neurons that can influence our emotions – hence the expression 'gut feelings'. Serotonin, which is involved in mood, is made in the gut and research suggests that healthy gut bacteria are linked to improved mood.

EATING FERMENTED FOOD TO PREVENT ILLNESS

Much research is being carried out to discover if eating probiotic foods can improve the health of people with specific disorders, and a number of studies have shown that beneficial bacteria may decrease the occurrence, duration and severity of certain illnesses and diseases, particularly those of the digestive system or immune system. These include inflammatory bowel disease (IBD), gastrointestinal inflammation and permeability (leaky gut syndrome), irritable bowel syndrome (IBS), viral gastroenteritis, antibiotic-associated diarrhoea, coeliac disease and food intolerances.

Gastro-related problems

The gastrointestinal or digestive tract (gut) is essentially a tube up to 9m (29.5 feet) long and its role is to break down food into the nutrients we need for energy, growth and repair. Many disorders can be relieved, treated or even prevented by dietary measures.

Coeliac disease is caused by sensitivity to gluten, a protein found in cereals, especially wheat, but also rye, barley and oats. The small intestine becomes inflamed and unable to absorb nutrients, causing a range of symptoms, including pain and bloating. Coeliac disease is an autoimmune condition whereby the immune system mistakenly attacks healthy tissue. Switching to a gluten-free diet helps control the symptoms, and eating small amounts of fermented food and drinks will help heal your digestive system (this can take up to two years after starting a gluten-free diet). Avoid rejuvelac, which is made from sprouted wheat berries (grains), as it may contain traces of gluten.

Constipation is usually defined as passing bowel motions less than twice a week or straining to do so more than 25 per cent of the time. In many cases this is linked with a poor dietary intake of fibre or fluids. Adding fermented vegetables and drinks to your diet (in addition to vegetables and beverages you already consume) should help as they have a mild laxative effect. A persistent change in bowel habit, especially in someone over the age of forty, should always be reported to a doctor to rule out the possibility of a more serious underlying factor.

Crohn's disease is a long-term condition that causes inflammation of the lining of the digestive system, and swelling and ulceration of the bowel wall. People with Crohn's can go for long periods without symptoms or with very mild symptoms, which include diarrhoea, abdominal pain, fatigue and unintended weight loss. A combination of factors may be responsible for triggering Crohn's, including genetics, a faulty immune system, previous infection or environmental factors; it is most common in Western countries and least common in poorer parts of the world such as Africa (this is known as the hygiene hypothesis). Although diet can't cure Crohn's, making sensible food choices can reduce some of the symptoms and it's a good idea to keep a food diary to see which foods work for you and discover what triggers flare-ups. Adding fermented foods and drinks to your diet between flare-ups can help (but not during flare-ups, as they have a mild laxative effect). Choose sugar-free dairy products such as yogurt and kefir as these reintroduce healthy bacteria to the gut.

Inflammatory bowel disease (IBD) is a term used to describe two conditions: Crohn's disease and ulcerative colitis, a similar illness which only affects the colon (large intestine). Some people with ulcerative colitis need to have part of their bowl removed and a loop of bowel constructed to replace this. This loop (or pouch) can become inflamed and when this happens it is known as 'pouchitis'. Studies have shown that adding a prescribed probiotic preparation to drinks or yogurts can help treat this.

Gastroenteritis means inflammation of the stomach or intestines and is a term used to describe food poisoning. It is usually caused by eating or drinking contaminated food or liquids. It may be a viral or bacterial infection or due to toxins such as those produced by staphylococcal bacteria. Symptoms include stomach pains, vomiting and diarrhoea and show between one and twelve hours if the illness is due to bacterial toxins and between twelve and forty-eight hours if due to a bacterial or viral infection. Regularly eating foods containing beneficial bacteria, such as lactobacilli in yogurt, can help to keep food poisoning at bay, by fighting 'bad' bacteria. There is also some evidence that consuming a small amount of non-dairy cultured food or drink, for example a few spoonfuls of Coconut Yogurt (page 52) or Coconut Milk Kefir (page 64) or Water Kefir (page 70), can shorten an episode of diarrhoea caused by a stomach bug by about a day.

Irritable bowel syndrome (IBS) is a common condition to affect the gut. It causes intermittent abdominal discomfort and often bloating, constipation or diarrhoea. To relieve IBS it's important to eat as many different sources of fibre as possible, including complex (unrefined) carbohydrates such as wholegrain bread and unsweetened wholegrain breakfast cereals. Eating a range of fermented foods, particularly yogurt, which contains lactobacilli can improve symptoms in some sufferers. This is supported by research published in 2010, although the extent of the benefits has yet to be determined.

Lactose intolerance is caused by deficiency of a metabolic enzyme known as lactase, which is needed to digest lactose (milk sugar) before it can be absorbed. The enzyme is released from the lining of the small intestine and breaks down lactose into two sugars, glucose and galactose, which are then immediately absorbed into the bloodstream. Those suffering from lactase deficiency experience unpleasant symptoms including abdominal pain, bloating and diarrhoea. The deficiency can be present from birth or may result temporarily after a bout of gastroenteritis. It is therefore usual to advise that those with diarrhoea (especially children) should avoid milk until symptoms have improved. Studies have found that non-dairy fermented foods containing *Lactobacillus acidophilus*, such as Coconut Drinking Yogurt (page 54), may reduce the symptoms of lactose intolerance.

Leaky gut syndrome is a condition in which the mucosal barrier (the barrier between the inside of the gut and the rest of the body, which absorbs nutrients but prevents most large molecules and bacteria passing from inside the bowel into the bloodstream) becomes less effective and 'leaky'. There is some disagreement among the medical profession, but exponents of leaky gut syndrome believe the bowel lining becomes leaky as a result of an overgrowth of undesirable yeasts and bacteria and excessive intake of 'inflammatory' foods such as gluten, sugar and alcohol, and that reinoculating with beneficial bacteria can help heal the mucosal barrier.

Weight-loss treatment and the illnesses associated with being overweight cost the UK more than 6 billion pounds a year. More than a third of men and women are overweight and more than 20 per cent of those are obese, i.e. have a BMI (Body Mass Index) – which is calculated as a ratio of weight to height – of above 30. Obesity has a huge impact on health, and the National Audit Office has suggested that in England alone there are more than 30,000 deaths a year resulting from obesity. Being obese increases your risk of diabetes and of cardiovascular diseases, including heart disease, high blood pressure and stroke. It also increases your risk of gall-bladder disease, sleep apnoea, osteoarthritis and certain cancers, including breast, colon and prostate.

We know that there are a number of genes that influence both weight and appetite and while good bacteria can't change these, they can modify their activity. It's now thought that the diversity and balance of our individual microbes have an effect on how hungry we feel and how fat is stored. Experiments have shown that obese and slim people often have very different populations of bacteria in their gut and more importantly that the type of bacteria pre-disposes us to obesity rather than the other way round. Research on several pairs of identical twins, in which one was obese and the other a normal weight, showed that in each case the slimmer twin had a greater diversity and more beneficial microbes in their gut. Although much more research is needed, it is clear that the key to a healthy weight lies not just in the amount of calories you consume, but also in the diversity and numbers of microbes in the gut.

Other illness and disease

In 2017 research in the field of neuroscience, published in the journal *Frontiers*, showed that a yogurt with probiotic bacteria can help improve symptoms of Alzheimer's. Although the disease is incurable, research indicated there were 'moderate but significant' improvements in Alzheimer's patients. Current research is exploring whether beneficial bacteria can help prevent or improve other conditions such as diabetes, autism and autoimmune diseases such as HIV, rheumatoid arthritis and multiple sclerosis. While there are many studies, books and blogs written on the subject, claiming that beneficial bacteria and fermented foods can improve all these ailments, there is no conclusive scientific evidence yet.

CHOOSE YOUR INGREDIENTS

You will find more information about specific ingredients needed for fermenting vegetables, dairy and drinks in the relevant chapters. Generally, ingredients should be as fresh as possible and unadulterated, i.e. free of additives. Where possible, choose organic for fresh ingredients such as milk, fruit and vegetables as these will be free of antibiotics and preservatives that will slow or prevent the beneficial bacteria thriving.

Salt

Salt plays a pivotal role in vegetable and fruit fermentation by creating conditions that favour beneficial bacteria (lactic acid bacteria can tolerate high salt concentrations) while preventing the growth of undesirable micro-organisms. At the same time, it extracts moisture from the food, making fermented vegetables and pickles crisper as well as adding flavour. Massaging the vegetables with salt (as in sauerkraut and other cabbage-based ferments) breaks down cell walls and releases juices to make brine. Pure unrefined sea salt is the best type to use in fermentation and this can be in the form of flakes or crystals. Much depends on how quickly you need the salt to dissolve, but generally flakes and smaller crystals are easier to use. Sea salt is produced through the evaporation of ocean water or saltwater lakes and will also provide some trace minerals, including magnesium. The crystals may be slightly grey in colour rather than pure white, although this will rarely be a problem when diluted with water. You can buy many speciality types of crystal salt, such as pink Himalayan salt, but these tend to be too expensive to use in fermenting vegetables as you will not be able to detect the flavour or colour.

Table salt can be used to make pickles and ferments, provided it only contains 'salt' on the ingredients list, so check labels carefully. Mined from underground salt deposits, it is highly processed to remove undesirable minerals and usually contains additives to prevent it clumping, and sometimes added minerals such as iodine – a useful additive as it is essential for the thyroid gland, which produces hormones that control many of the body's functions. However, these additives can taint the flavour of pickles and may make them cloudy.

Traditionally, vegetables have been fermented with a lot of salt because ferments with less salt are more prone to mould. Salt also slows down the fermentation process, which allows flavour to develop more slowly, resulting in better-tasting produce. Today, nutritionists recommend reducing the amount of salt we eat, so serve your pickles and ferments with less salty foods and when using them in recipes, adjust seasonings accordingly. The amount of salt in pickles and ferments can be reduced a little depending on personal taste and the types of vegetables. If you reduce it, add a little whey (page 50) or juices from a previous ferment to compensate and to speed up the initial growth of beneficial bacteria. Once your ferment is complete, taste the vegetables; if they are a little too salty, remove a small amount of the fermenting juice (use it to start another batch) and replace with cooled boiled water.

Making brine

Most recipes give a quantity of salt, but as some vegetables may have lost moisture during storage or may have been grown during dry weather, less liquid may be extracted during salting, meaning extra could be needed to submerge the contents in the jar: this is vital to prevent the growth of mould. If only a small amount of liquid is needed, you can add a little filtered water, but if more than 2.5cm (1in) of vegetables remains uncovered, you will need to add brine. The concentration of brine can be varied but a concentration of 6 per cent salt by weight is ideal for most fermented vegetables. Put 15g (½oz) crystal sea salt or sea salt flakes in a small pan and pour over 150ml (¼ pint) filtered water. Gently heat, stirring occasionally until the salt has dissolved. Remove from the heat and pour in a further 100ml (4fl oz) cold filtered water. Leave to cool completely before using. The brine can be stored in a bottle or jar in the fridge for up to six months. You can make a larger or smaller quantity of brine, but keep the proportions the same, allowing 1g salt for every 15ml (1 tbsp) filtered water. Check the top of the fermenting vegetables daily and if there is any evidence of mould, remove it immediately and add a few spoonfuls of brine to reduce the chances of the ferment spoiling.

Sugar

Organic sugar is recommended when making fermented food. This is because it is important to avoid chemical additives and any traces of pesticides when making fermented food, as these may interfere with the growth of beneficial bacteria. Regulations vary from country to country, but generally 'organic' means that the sugar was grown organically, and made through the first sugar crystallisation without the application of any synthetic chemicals or additions. When producing organic sugar, the sugar cane juice will still contain tiny amounts of molasses, vitamins and minerals, and when evaporated and crystallised will result in a pale golden sugar. If you can't find any sugar labelled 'organic' look for the words 'natural' or 'golden' instead. Don't confuse this with 'light brown' sugar as many brands are made by coating highly refined white sugar with molasses, meaning the sugar crystals are only brown on the outside.

Molasses

This thick, dark, heavy syrup is a by-product of sugar refining. Highly nutritious, it contains all the minerals and nutrients absorbed by the plant, including iron, calcium and magnesium. It can be used instead of dried fruit when making Water Kefir (page 70) and provides the kefir with nutrients to keep it living and growing indefinitely. Molasses will make the water kefir and the crystals straw-coloured, rather than white.

Water

This is a vital ingredient when fermenting vegetables and fruit and is usually mixed with salt to make brine. You can buy spring (bottled) water, but as this is expensive, filtered tap water is recommended in the recipes in this book. Tap water is usually chlorinated by water authorities to prevent the growth of all microbes. Some add a related chemical known as chloramines, which is more difficult to remove as it is bound with ammonia. You can find out how much chlorine and chloramines is in your water by looking online at the water report from the supplier for your area. As beneficial microbes are necessary for fermentation, it is important to remove as much chlorine, chloramines and other additives as possible, either by using a filter jug (change the filter cartridge regularly), the easiest and a fairly inexpensive method, or one of the following:

- Boil the water for two to three minutes and then leave it to cool. The chlorine and most of the chloramines will boil out of the water and evaporate.
- Leave the water in an open bowl for twenty-four hours; this allows the chlorine to evaporate. It works less well with chloramines.
- Use a reverse osmosis filter. Although this is an expensive piece of equipment, it purifies water better than any of the other methods,

removing a wide range of contaminants, including chlorine and chloramines, pesticides, heavy metals and other pollutants.

EQUIPMENT

When you begin making fermented foods and drinks, having the correct equipment for the job will make the whole process easier and help to ensure success. You will probably have most of the basic items, but a few specific items such as airlock jars, a plastic sieve and some muslin will prove invaluable. The following is a brief outline of the most useful items, all of which are readily available online and from large department stores and specialist kitchen equipment stores.

Jars and crocks

Only use fermenting jars and crocks sold specifically for fermentation (often labelled 'pickling' jars) as these should be safe and thick enough for the process. Use wide-mouth jars to make packing of vegetables easy; most recipes in the following chapters use a 1 litre (1¾ pint) fermenting jar, although you can use two 500ml (17fl oz) jars instead or choose to make a half or double quantity of recipes. Avoid metal containers such as aluminium, copper and tin as these will react with the acids in fermenting foods. Plastic containers are not recommended as they can harbour harmful bacteria and may also react with the fermented food and leach chemicals.

Airlock jars

These are glass preserving jars with a lid containing an airlock that allows carbon dioxide gas to safely vent through its seal while preventing any undesirable bacteria entering. The seal is designed to create a layer of carbon dioxide gas in the space between the fermenting food and the lid to inhibit growth of mould (it's therefore important not to remove the lid during the fermentation process). The jars and lids are reusable, so they are an excellent investment for safe and successful fermentation.

Fermenting crocks

Traditional fermenting crocks are usually dark brown ceramic, although more vibrantly coloured ones are now available. They are ideal when making larger quantities and range in size from 2 litres to a massive 20 litres (3½ to 35 pints). The main advantage is that the thick stoneware walls create a stable fermentation temperature and may allow a greater range and number of beneficial bacteria to develop. The disadvantage of using this over an airlock jar is that the sealed environment makes it harder to monitor what is going on inside.

There are two types of fermentation crocks: open and water-sealed. In an open crock, the vegetables and brine are added and a plate is placed inside to hold whatever is being fermented below the brine. A cloth is then secured over the opening. It is an easy way to ferment, but because ferments such as sauerkraut are best done in an anaerobic (without air) environment, it is not uncommon for the ferment to develop surface mould and it can be difficult to prevent fruit flies being attracted to the fermenting food. Water-sealed crocks are slightly more sophisticated; they usually have two half-circle weights to keep the ferment submerged. The lid is then placed on to an open 'moat', a large deep channel inside the top edge of the jar which is filled with water. This provides a seal and prevents air from entering the crock, while allowing carbon dioxide created during fermentation to bubble out. The water moat must be monitored and refilled when necessary (as some of the water will evaporate) to maintain the seal.

The bases of most earthenware crocks are not glazed, so it is important to protect your floor, shelf or work surface from condensation by raising the crock up slightly or by placing it on a board.

Pickle weights

These heavy round glass weights are also called pickle pebbles and are made from lead-free non-porous glass. They are designed to fit regular and wide-mouth mason jars and keep the fermenting vegetables well below the brine. It is also possible to buy larger stone weights to fit fermenting crocks; these are usually two half-moons which fit together to make a circle. There are other ways of holding your vegetables under the brine, such as a heavy plate (sterilise in the dishwasher first); a folded cabbage leaf is the traditional way of keeping sauerkraut submerged.

Vegetable pounders

Also known as 'stompers' or 'tampers', these can be used to extract liquid from cabbage and other vegetables directly in a crock, instead of massaging the cabbage with your hands. Salted cabbage can be added to the crock in small layers, then gently bashed with the pounder to soften and compact it.

Tampers are usually wooden and you should choose one made with heavy, dense wood such as maple as it will be more resistant to abrasion and wear. Hand-wash thoroughly after use and allow to air-dry before storing. The wood should occasionally be treated with a protective coat of 'butcher block conditioner', a food-grade mineral oil, which will prevent it from drying and cracking.

Sieves, colanders and spoons

You will need a plastic sieve to strain fermented drinks such as milk and water kefir, and for making kombucha and rejuvelac and straining yogurt to make Greek yogurt or fresh cheeses such as labneh. Some fermenters say that stainless steel is fine if only in brief contact with fermented products, but generally metal should be avoided as it can destroy beneficial bacteria and give a faint metallic taste to the finished product. You should also use a plastic or stainless steel colander when making fermented vegetables and fruit, for the same reasons. Metal spoons should not be used for fermented dairy and drinks; instead use wooden spoons, preferably new or specifically kept for this purpose, to avoid cross-contamination.

Bowls

Essential for salting, soaking and mixing, you can use glass or plastic bowls for making fermented vegetables and fruit. Glass is preferable as plastic bowls are more likely to absorb undesirable microbes. Make sure your bowl is heatproof, so that you can sterilise it, either with boiling water (always rinse out with warm water first so there isn't a massive heat change, which might crack the bowl) or in the dishwasher on a hot cycle.

Chopping boards

Whether you choose plastic or wooden chopping boards, it's important to keep them scrupulously clean. Plastic boards can usually be washed and sterilised in the dishwasher, but some prefer wood as it is less likely to dull knives and is considered a natural product. Whichever you pick, wash it well and – if you don't use a dishwasher – dry with a clean tea towel, then leave to air-dry standing on its side (as germs breed on damp surfaces). It is preferable to use a new board and keep it for fermented foods or one that has been used for chopping vegetables only (not meat or fish).

Thermometer

Yogurt-making bacteria need the temperature 'just right' and a digital thermometer with a thin stainless steel probe is ideal, as the probe can be sterilised by rinsing in boiling water (allow to cool before using to ensure an accurate reading).

STERILISING EQUIPMENT

Before fermenting, it is essential to sterilise equipment, jars and bottles to destroy any undesirable micro-organisms, as these could cause the fermented food or drink to deteriorate or become inedible. Sterilising is important for all containers, but you should take particular care when reusing jars and bottles previously used for a different food. Check jars and bottles for damage or cracks, then wash thoroughly in hot soapy water (do not use an anti-bacterial washing-up liquid as any residue could destroy beneficial bacteria when fermenting), then rinse well and turn upside down to drain. Do not use any cleaning agents such as sterilising tablets or disinfectants as these will both taint the fermented food or drink and prevent beneficial bacteria multiplying. Glass jars and bottles may be sterilised in several different ways:

- **Oven method** Stand the containers, spaced slightly apart, on a baking sheet lined with kitchen paper. Rest any lids on top. Place in a cold oven, then heat to 110°C (fan 100°C), gas ¼, and leave in the oven for 30 minutes. Leave to cool. If the jars or bottles are not used immediately, cover with a clean cloth.
- **Boiling water method** Place the containers, open-end up, in a deep pan that is wide enough to hold them in one layer. Pour enough hot water into the pan to fill and cover the containers (do not use boiling water as this can crack cold glass). Bring the water to the boil and boil for 10 minutes. Leave the containers in the pan until the water stops bubbling, then carefully remove and drain upside down on a clean tea towel. Turn the containers upright and leave to air-dry. Immerse the lids in simmering water for 20 seconds.
- **Microwave method** This can only be used for short squat bottles or containers that will fit in the microwave. Half fill the clean jars or bottles with warm water and heat on full power until the water has boiled for at least one minute. Open the door and let the bottles cool for a minute or two, then remove using oven gloves. Carefully swirl the water inside, then tip it away. Drain upside down on a clean tea towel, then turn upright and leave to dry.
- **Dishwasher method** This is the simplest way to clean and sterilise, especially if you have a large number of bottles, jars and other equipment. Put the containers and lids in the dishwasher and run it on its hottest setting including drying. If the containers and equipment are already clean, you can run the cycle without adding detergent.

Sterilising other equipment

Providing they are dishwasher-proof, knives, bowls, jugs and plastic chopping boards can all be sterilised by washing in a dishwasher on its hottest setting. Knives that aren't suitable for the dishwasher can be sterilised by placing in a heatproof jug (at least as tall as the blade) and pouring over boiling water to cover the blade, then leaving for 2 minutes. Wipe dry on kitchen paper before using. Rinse items such as wooden spoons in boiling water, even if new.

SIMPLE STEPS FOR SAFE FERMENTING

Food poisoning from fermented foods is very rare and following a few simple rules will ensure that fermented foods are safe to eat. The first four steps apply to all fermenting, whether vegetables, dairy or fermented beverages. Steps five to eight apply specifically to fermenting vegetables.

1. **Keep it clean** Make sure everything you use in the fermenting process is clean. This means sterilising jars, bottles, bowls and other tools and thoroughly washing your hands. The same rule applies when tasting your pickles and ferments and if you choose to transfer them to other jars or bottles before storing in the fridge.
2. **Watch the temperature** Gut-friendly bacteria thrive best at certain temperatures, but will die off if it gets too hot. Follow advice in individual recipes about temperature and keep ferments out of direct sunlight. In warmer weather, move your ferments to a cooler room or cupboard.
3. **Check acid level** Foods with a low acid level are more hospitable to bad bacteria and spoilage. Fermented food should have a pH of 4.6 or lower. You can buy pH strips to test this to ensure the levels are safe.
4. **Check frequently** Use your common sense. While removing a small amount of mould growing on the top of fermented vegetables may save the produce and allow beneficial bacteria to fight off the mould, once this happens the spores may spread and spoil the ferment, so you need to check more regularly. If the mould reappears or if a vegetable ferment darkens, becomes pink or has a creamy film on top, or if a dairy ferment smells odd, yeasty or cheesy, it has spoiled and you need to discard it and start again.
5. **Use sufficient salt and/or brine** Too little salt gives undesirable bacteria and yeasts the opportunity to grow on the surface. It is preferable to keep to a concentration of 6 per cent salt. If any mould or scum appears on the surface, you must spoon it off and remove the fermenting vegetables immediately below the scum as they may contain mould spores, then top up the ferment with more brine (page 10). As a rule of thumb, there should always be 2.5cm (1in) brine above the vegetables.

6 **Weight it down** When fermenting vegetables and fruit, it's vital to keep the ingredients under brine. Vegetables that float to the top will be exposed to air and could pick up 'bad' bacteria.
7 **Don't overfill or underfill jars** The fermentation process needs space to bubble, so leave at least 2.5cm (1in) between the brine and the top of the jar. You should also fill the jars sufficiently; less than 75 per cent full will leave too much room for oxygen, which may contain microbes which spoil the ferment.
8 **Seal it** If possible, make vegetable ferments in a sealed jar or crock as oxygen increases the risk of mould. Jars with airlocks or water-sealed fermenting crocks are recommended, as they keep out oxygen but allow fermenting gases to escape.

> **Note**
> Fermented food and drinks are not suitable for those who have severe allergies to moulds.

GETTING STARTED

Fermented foods and beverages should be part of a well-balanced diet, so start by making healthy choices with nutrient-rich foods and reducing your intake of processed and sugary foods. It takes a little time for your body to adjust to fermented foods, so start slowly and don't eat large amounts in one go as they may have a mild laxative effect. Begin with a small portion once a day, then gradually build up the quantity to give your gut microbiota the chance to adjust. Include a variety of fermented foods and beverages in your diet, as each will give your gut a mix of different micro-organisms. You will soon start enjoying the flavours and health benefits of fermented food.

CHAPTER 2

Fermenting Vegetables and Fruit

You can ferment with just vegetables, salt and filtered or non-chlorinated water, or you can speed up the fermenting process by adding a starter culture. In this chapter you'll find both methods used. Almost any vegetable, and some fruits, can be fermented, but cabbage is probably the most widely known fermented preserve and is the basis of both sauerkraut and kimchi.

The most suitable and successful vegetables for fermenting have a firm texture and relatively low sugar content. They include green leafy vegetables such as cabbage and pak choi, and root vegetables such as radishes, kohlrabi and turnips. Vegetables, such as carrots and peppers are excellent for adding both flavour and colour and work well when mixed with cruciferous vegetables. Slightly temperamental fermenters include cucumbers and summer squashes such as courgettes, as they have a high water content, and produce such as beetroot, parsnip, apples and pears, which have a higher sugar content. A starter culture should be used with these to boost the fermentation process.

TOP TIPS FOR FERMENTING VEGETABLES AND FRUIT

- Choose organic produce if possible because non-organic may contain traces of chemicals that may impede the fermenting process. Buying organic is particularly important when you plan to eat the rind, peel or skin or if you are buying types which either get a lot of pesticides applied to them or tend to absorb pesticides, for example carrots, peppers and apples. Non-organic vegetables should be peeled and leafy vegetables have their outer leaves removed.

- Produce should be at the peak of freshness; if possible, choose food grown locally and in season.
- Vegetables and fruit can be sliced, grated or left whole, but bear in mind that larger, thicker pieces will take longer to ferment. The smaller you cut them, the more surface area there is for the bacteria to inhabit, and smaller pieces will allow you to pack more into the jars. If you are using a mixture of vegetables, cut into similar even-sized slices or pieces.
- Vegetables and fruit culture best at room temperature: around 22°C (72°F) is ideal. Above that temperature speeds up the process; below will slow it down. Find a spot where your jars can sit undisturbed out of direct sunlight. If your kitchen is very sunny, put the bottles in a cardboard box to keep out the light.
- Do not open or unscrew the jars for the first three days to keep oxygen out during the start of the fermentation process. After that time, you can check daily, removing a small amount with a clean fork.
- For a more sour taste, continue fermenting, testing every few days. The more sour the taste, the more beneficial bacteria are present. You may find your taste buds change and you start to crave more strongly flavoured and developed preserves.
- Transfer the finished jars to the fridge as soon as they are ready. This will considerably slow the fermentation process. 'Burp' the jars weekly by unscrewing the lid, closing firmly, then loosening by a quarter turn, to release the small amount of gas that your live preserve will continue to produce.

USING A STARTER CULTURE

A starter culture contains living beneficial organisms in dry or liquid form that provide the food with an active colony of microbes to encourage and speed up the fermentation process. 'Good' fermenters such as cabbage do not usually need a starter as they naturally attract the right sorts of microbes, but others can benefit from a little help. There are three basic types of starter:

1. **Liquid from fermented vegetables** This can either be shop-bought (but make sure it contains live beneficial bacteria), or from

a previous batch of home-made fermented vegetables such as sauerkraut. The amount you use depends on what you are fermenting; sometimes just a few spoonfuls is enough; anything up to 150ml (¼ pint) can be added.

2 **Live dairy whey from yogurt** Whey is the thin watery liquid from either strained yogurt or after milk has been curdled and strained when making cheese. You can often find it on the top of a pot of plain yogurt; carefully pour this off and use it. Simple to make (see page 50), it can be frozen for up to two months without harming the beneficial micro-organisms. Whey is a pale yellow clearish liquid, so won't affect the appearance of the finished product. Kefir can also be used in the same way, but it is milky-coloured and opaque and will make the preserving liquid cloudy. Using live dairy means the preserve won't be suitable for vegans.

3 **Vegetable fermentation starter culture** This powder is usually sold in small sachets and although more expensive than other options, tends to produce consistent and reliable results. The culture may or may not contain dairy.

SEASONINGS, SPICES AND FLAVOURS

Apart from salt, which plays an important role in the fermentation process, as well as acting as a seasoning, there is a huge range of flavourings which you can add to your preserves.

- Caraway seeds and juniper berries are traditional flavourings in many European preserves, especially sauerkraut. You can leave them out of recipes if you don't like the flavour or try similar ones such as fennel or anise seeds.
- Dill is a classic seasoning in sour preserves such as cucumber pickles. Fronds of fennel have a similar flavour and appearance.
- 'Pickling spices' are usually intended for vinegar-based pickles such as pickled onions, but they can be used in fermented preserves too. Usually they contain a blend of allspice, clove, cinnamon, bay leaf, ginger, black pepper and turmeric and may add colour as well as flavour. Use small quantities when trying for the first time as the flavour can be overpowering.

- Vinegar can be added in small quantities to increase the acidity of the finished preserve. Choose red wine vinegar or cider vinegar and add no more than 60ml (4 tbsp) per 1 litre (1¾ pint) jar. The vinegar must be boiled first, then cooled.
- Ingredients containing tannin are often added to preserves to keep the vegetables crunchy and to inhibit certain enzymes in vegetables such as cucumbers. Try topping your preserve with a couple of fresh oak or grape leaves, or add a tea bag containing black tea at the bottom of your jar.
- You may wish to reduce the amount of salt in pickles (especially if you are trying to stick to a low-salt diet), but shouldn't cut it out completely as salt inhibits the growth of mould and acts as a preservative. Cut the quantity in recipes by no more than a third and add some starter to compensate and speed up the fermenting process.

Simple Sauerkraut, Step by Step

Sauerkraut, which means 'sour cabbage', is an everyday food in many parts of Eastern Europe. While it is sometimes flavoured with aromatic spices such as caraway seeds and peppercorns, in its basic form it contains only two ingredients: cabbage and salt. It can be eaten after just five days, when it is still crunchy and just slightly sour, or left until it has a comfortingly soft texture and a more pronounced acidity, perfect for serving with rich meats and strongly flavoured cheeses.

The detailed steps in this basic recipe can be applied to all the other fermented vegetable and fruit recipes in this chapter.

MAKES ABOUT 500G (JUST OVER 1LB)

1 firm pale green or white cabbage, weighing about 900g (2lb)
20g (¾oz) coarse crystal sea salt or flakes

1 Remove the outer two or three leaves from the cabbage and discard (or use in another recipe). Cut the cabbage into quarters and remove some of the tough central core. Shred the cabbage very finely, either by hand with a large sharp knife or in a food processor, using a slicing disc. Layer the cabbage and salt in a very clean bowl (rinse out the bowl – make sure it's heatproof – with boiling water from the kettle first to kill any undesirable bacteria), then using clean hands firmly massage the cabbage for 5 minutes. The cabbage will feel tough and squeaky at first, but will gradually soften and start to ooze juices.

2 Leave for 5 minutes so that the salt can draw out a little more liquid and soften the cabbage, then massage again for 3–4 minutes; you should now have a much-reduced volume of cabbage in its own briny juices.

3 If you don't have any specialist fermenting bottles with airlocks (see page 12), cover the surface of the cabbage entirely with a sheet of cling film, pressing out any air bubbles. Weigh down the cabbage so that it sits beneath the brine, using a plate which just fits inside the bowl and a couple of weights or small food tins.

Cover the top of the bowl with more cling film and leave at cool room temperature, about 18°C (64°F). (Some preserves are better fermented more quickly at a slightly higher temperature, but cabbage on its own benefits from a slow ferment.)

4 If you are not using fermenting bottles with airlocks, check the cabbage every day or so and release any gas bubbles that have built up under the cling film. Push the bubbles to the sides of the cling film, then lift up the edges to release them; try not to open up completely to the air. However, if there is any scum on top, peel the cling film back and remove with a spoon (first rinsed under boiling water). Try to keep the fermenting sauerkraut at an even temperature – too warm and it may become mouldy; too cool and it will take a long time to ferment.

5 If you prefer, you can spoon the massaged cabbage straight away into a sterilised 1 litre (1¾ pint) jar, leaving a 5cm (2in) fermenting space at the top of the jar. The cabbage should have produced enough brine of its own; if not, add enough brine (page 10) to ensure the cabbage is completely submerged. Use the base of a small clean glass to pack the mixture down one last time. Put on the lid, close firmly, and then loosen by a quarter turn. Leave the jars at room temperature out of direct sunlight for 7 days. After day 3, 'burp' the jar each day by unscrewing the lid, closing firmly, then loosening by a quarter turn.

6 The cabbage will be ready to eat or you can leave it to ferment for longer, up to 4 weeks, or until the bubbling subsides. Taste the sauerkraut after 6–7 days, then every couple of days until it is to your liking. If you have made the sauerkraut in a bowl, transfer to sterilised jars and store in the fridge for up to 4 months.

Note
It's important to keep the cabbage completely covered with brine. If you don't have pickle weights or a suitable plate or saucer, use the outer cabbage leaves you removed, roll up and use to wedge the sauerkraut down. Discard these when the sauerkraut has finished fermenting and before you put it in the fridge.

Spiced Red Cabbage and Apple Sauerkraut

Caraway seeds and juniper berries are classic sauerkraut spices. Here they add an aromatic flavour to crisp and tangy red cabbage combined with juicy apples.

MAKES ABOUT 900G (2LB)

1 red cabbage, weighing about 750g (1¾lb)
20g (¾oz) fine sea salt
1 apple, quartered, peeled, cored and coarsely chopped
10ml (2 tsp) caraway seeds
15ml (1 tbsp) juniper berries, crushed

1 Remove the outer two or three leaves from the cabbage and discard (or use in another recipe). Cut the cabbage into quarters and remove some of the tough central core. Shred the cabbage very finely, either by hand or in a food processor. Layer the cabbage and salt in a bowl, then firmly massage the cabbage for 5 minutes. Leave for 5 minutes, then massage again for 2–3 minutes; you should now have a much-reduced volume of cabbage in its own briny juices.

2 Add the apple, caraway seeds and juniper berries. Mix together thoroughly. Tightly pack the mixture into a sterilised 1 litre (1¾ pint) glass jar, pressing down firmly.

3 Use the base of a small clean glass to pack down the mixture one last time, leaving a 5cm (2in) fermenting space at the top of the jar. The cabbage should have produced enough brine of its own; if not, add enough brine (page 10) to ensure the cabbage is completely submerged.

4 Put on the lid, close firmly, and then loosen by a quarter turn. Leave the jar at room temperature out of direct sunlight for 7 days. 'Burp' the jar each day by opening the lid, closing firmly, then loosening by a quarter turn. Taste after 7 days, then every couple of days after (up to 2 weeks), until to your liking. Store in the fridge for up to 3 months.

Mixed Vegetable Slaw

This fermented vegetable mixture is delicious tossed in a Carolina-style salad dressing to accompany grilled, barbecued or slow-cooked food such as pulled pork, spicy chicken or veggie-burgers. Store the dressing separately and mix with the vegetables just before serving. This is also good served with yogurt dressing (page 113).

MAKES ABOUT 900G (2LB)

1 small firm light green or white cabbage, weighing about 800g (1lb 13oz)
20g (¾oz) crystal sea salt
1 red onion, peeled, halved and thinly sliced
1 red pepper, quartered, deseeded and thinly sliced
2 carrots, peeled and cut into fine matchstick strips
2.5ml (½ tsp) celery seeds

For the dressing
2.5ml (½ tsp) dry mustard powder
15ml (1 tbsp) clear honey
90ml (6 tbsp) sunflower oil
15ml (1 tbsp) apple cider vinegar
freshly ground black pepper

1 Remove the outer two or three leaves from the cabbage and discard (or use in another recipe). Cut the cabbage into quarters and remove some of the tough central core. Shred the cabbage very finely, either by hand or in a food processor. Layer the cabbage and salt in a bowl, then firmly massage the cabbage for 5 minutes. Leave for 5 minutes, then massage again for 2–3 minutes; you should now have a much-reduced volume of cabbage in its own briny juices.

2. Add the red onion, pepper, carrots and celery seeds. Mix together thoroughly. Tightly pack the mixture into a sterilised 1 litre (1¾ pint) glass jar, pressing down firmly.
3. Use a small clean glass to pack down the mixture one last time, leaving a 5cm (2in) fermenting space at the top of the jar. The cabbage should have produced enough brine of its own; if not, add brine (page 10) to ensure the mixture is completely submerged.
4. Put on the lid, close firmly, and then loosen by a quarter turn. Leave the jar at room temperature out of direct sunlight for 7 days. 'Burp' the jar each day by opening the lid, closing firmly, then loosening by a quarter turn. Taste after 7 days, then every couple of days after (up to 2 weeks), until to your liking. Store in the fridge for up to 2 months.
5. When the slaw has fermented, make the dressing. Blend the mustard powder and honey together in a small bowl. Slowly whisk in the oil, followed by the vinegar, then season to taste with black pepper. Store in a small screw-top jar in the fridge for up to 2 months.
6. When ready to serve, spoon as much slaw as you require into a colander and drain off most of the liquid. Tip the slaw into a bowl and drizzle over enough of the dressing to taste. Mix thoroughly and serve.

Dill Pickles

In America jars of 'cucumber pickles' are such a quintessential fermented food, they are simply known as 'pickles' and are traditionally eaten with salt beef. The 'cucumbers' are small thick-skinned Lebanese cucumbers, which are known in the UK as gherkins and are picked when around 7.5cm (3in) long. Fresh ones are difficult to purchase here, but you can grow your own from seed.

MAKES ABOUT 900G (2LB)

about 900g (2lb) fresh gherkins (thick-skinned mini 'pickling' cucumbers)
40g (1½oz) crystal sea salt
750ml (1¼ pints) filtered water
150ml (¼ pint) whey (page 50) or sauerkraut juice
few sprigs of fresh dill
fresh grape leaf or oak leaf or a black tea bag (optional)

1 Cut a thin sliver off the flowering end of the gherkins and discard. Add the salt to the water and stir until dissolved. Stir in the whey or sauerkraut juice.
2 Put the dill at the bottom of a sterilised 1 litre (1¾ pint) pickle jar with the grape leaf, oak leaf or tea bag, if using. Add the gherkins, packing them tightly together.
3 Pour enough of the salted water over the gherkins to just cover, leaving a 5cm (2in) fermenting space at the top of the jar. Add a glass pickling weight or a clean small saucer that fits inside the jar to keep the gherkins submerged.

4 Put on the lid, close firmly, and then loosen by a quarter turn. Leave the jar at room temperature out of direct sunlight for 3 days. 'Burp' the jar each day by opening the lid, closing firmly, then loosening by a quarter turn. Taste after 3 days (carefully remove and cut a slice off one of the gherkins, then return to the jar), then every day after (tasting the same gherkin each time), until to your liking. Store in the fridge for up to 3 months.

Notes
- It's important to cut off the tips at the end of the cucumbers that would produce flowers (the opposite end to where they have been cut from the plant), as these contain enzymes that can spoil the pickle.
- Adding a little whey or sauerkraut juice speeds up fermentation so that the pickles may be ready in just 3–4 days.
- Tannins from grape or oak leaves or black tea bags will help flavour the pickles and keep them crunchy.

Fermented Spring Vegetables

This is a colourful mix including dark green kale, which you should buy whole rather than ready-shredded if you can. If preferred, you can replace the courgette with a red or yellow pepper.

MAKES ABOUT 900G (2LB)

large piece of firm light green or white cabbage, weighing about 500g (1¼lb)
20g (¾oz) crystal sea salt
200g (7oz) kale leaves
2 carrots
1 yellow courgette (or green if you can't get a yellow one)

1. Remove the outer two or three leaves from the cabbage and discard. Shred the cabbage very finely, either by hand or in a food processor. Layer the cabbage and salt in a bowl, then firmly massage the cabbage for 5 minutes. Leave for 5 minutes.
2. Finely shred the kale leaves and add to the bowl. Mix and massage for 3–4 minutes; you should now have a much-reduced volume of cabbage and kale in their own briny juices. Leave to stand for a few more minutes while preparing the rest of the vegetables.
3. Peel the carrots, halve lengthways and cut into thin slices. Trim the courgette, halve lengthways and finely slice. Add both to the cabbage mixture and mix together thoroughly. Tightly pack the mixture into a sterilised 1 litre (1¾ pint) glass jar, pressing down firmly.
4. Use the base of a small clean glass to pack down the mixture one last time, leaving a 5cm (2in) fermenting space at the top of the jar. The cabbage and kale should have produced enough brine of their own; if not, add enough brine (page 10) to ensure the mixture is completely submerged.
5. If not using an airlock jar, put on the lid, close firmly, and then loosen by a quarter turn. Leave the jar at room temperature out of direct sunlight for 7 days. 'Burp' the jar each day by opening the lid, closing firmly, then loosening by a quarter turn. Taste after 7 days, then every couple of days after (up to 2 weeks), until to your liking. Store in the fridge for up to 3 months.

Cauliflower, Carrot and Pepper Pickles

This colourful vegetable pickle adds taste and texture to any meal. Cut the vegetables into even-sized pieces for the best results and arrange in layers of individual vegetables or mix everything together before packing in the jar.

MAKES ABOUT 900G (2LB)

750ml (1¼ pints) filtered water
30ml (2 tbsp) crystal sea salt
2 carrots, about 175g (6oz) in total, peeled and cut into thin 2.5cm (1in) matchstick strips
1 red pepper, quartered, deseeded and cut into thin strips
1 yellow pepper, quartered, deseeded and cut into thin strips
175g (6oz) cauliflower, broken into tiny florets

1 Stir the water and salt together until dissolved. Tightly pack the vegetables into a sterilised 1 litre (1¾ pint) jar. Add enough of the salted water to cover the vegetables, leaving a 5cm (2in) fermenting space at the top of the jar.
2 Press down the vegetables to completely submerge them and if you need to, add a glass pickling weight or a clean small saucer that fits inside the jar to keep them under the liquid.
3 Put on the lid, close firmly, and then loosen by a quarter turn. Leave the jar at room temperature out of direct sunlight for 7 days. 'Burp' the jar each day by opening the lid, closing firmly, then loosening by a quarter turn.
4 Taste after 7 days, then every couple of days after (up to 2 weeks), until to your liking. Store in the fridge for up to 2 months.

Pickled Radishes with Red Onion and Apple

Radishes have a relatively short season in the shops, so make the most of them when available by making this tasty pickle. It's also a good way of using a glut if you grow your own. Cumin seeds are optional here; they add a lovely spicy flavour, but if you prefer you can let the radishes take centre stage.

MAKES A 1 LITRE (1¾ PINT) JAR

about 35 medium-sized radishes, trimmed
2 small red onions, peeled
1 eating apple, quartered, peeled and cored
2 garlic cloves, peeled and crushed
5ml (1 tsp) cumin seeds (optional)
60ml (4 tbsp) whey (page 50)
about 300ml (½ pint) brine (page 10)

1 Cut the radishes into quarters. Thinly slice the onions and cut the apple into small pieces, about 1cm (½in). Put them in a large bowl along with the garlic, and sprinkle over the cumin seeds if using. Mix well, then tightly pack into a sterilised 1 litre (1¾ pint) jar.
2 Spoon in the whey, then pour in enough brine to cover the vegetables, leaving a 5cm (2in) fermenting space at the top of the jar. If necessary, add a glass pickling weight or a clean small saucer that fits inside the jar to keep the vegetables submerged.

3 Put on the lid, close firmly, and then loosen by a quarter turn. Leave the jar at room temperature out of direct sunlight for 3–5 days. 'Burp' the jar each day by opening the lid, closing firmly, then loosening by a quarter turn. Taste after 3 days, then every day after until to your liking. Store in the fridge for up to 2 months.

> **Note**
> Don't discard the radish tops; the peppery leaves are delicious steamed as a vegetable and are packed with vitamin C. Once the radishes are harvested, the leaves wilt quickly and don't keep long, so trim them off as soon as possible, then wash and store in the salad drawer of the fridge and use within a day or two.

Classic Kimchi

An essential part of the Korean diet, kimchi provides a combination of salty, sweet, spicy and sour flavours. There are hundreds of different types, but this one, known as 'baechu kimchi', made with Chinese leaf, is one of the most popular.

MAKES A 1 LITRE (1¾ PINT) JAR

1 small head of Chinese leaves (Chinese cabbage), finely shredded
1 red pepper, quartered, deseeded and thinly sliced
1 large carrot, peeled and coarsely grated
150g (5oz) radishes, thinly sliced
2.5cm (1in) piece fresh ginger, peeled and grated
2 spring onions, thinly sliced
20g (¾oz) sea salt flakes
10ml (2 tsp) fish sauce
10ml (2 tsp) gochugaru (Korean chilli powder, see Note)
filtered water, as needed

1 Put all the prepared vegetables in a large bowl, then sprinkle over the salt. Gently massage the vegetables for 5 minutes. Leave for 5 minutes.
2 Sprinkle over the fish sauce and chilli powder, then mix and massage again for 2–3 minutes; you should now have a much-reduced volume of vegetables in their own briny juices.
3 Pack the vegetables and brine into a sterilised 1 litre (1¾ pint) glass jar, packing down the vegetables so that they are completely submerged, leaving a 5cm (2in) fermenting space at the top of the jar. If there isn't enough liquid, add a little filtered water to cover.

4 Put on the lid, close firmly, and then loosen by a quarter turn. Leave the jar at room temperature out of direct sunlight for 7 days. 'Burp' the jar each day by opening the lid, closing firmly, then loosening by a quarter turn.
5 Taste after 7 days, then every couple of days after (up to 2 weeks), until to your liking. Store in the fridge for up to 3 months.

Note
If you can't get gochugaru (Korean chilli powder), use 5ml (1 tsp) chilli powder (hot or mild, whichever you prefer) and 5ml (1 tsp) smoked paprika.

Chunky Kimchi

Kimchi is the generic Korean name for pickled vegetables and there are hundreds of variations of this 'must have' accompaniment. This one, like most, includes Chinese leaves, cut into larger pieces rather than finely shredded, and crisp white mooli (daikon radish).

MAKES A 1 LITRE (1¾ PINT) JAR

1 small head of Chinese leaves (Chinese cabbage)
60ml (4 tbsp) sea salt flakes
4 garlic cloves
2.5cm (1in) piece fresh ginger
10ml (2 tsp) golden caster sugar
15ml (1 tbsp) gochugaru (Korean chilli powder, see Note page 35)
5ml (1 tsp) fish sauce
200g (7oz) mooli (daikon radish)
6–8 spring onions

For the brine
5ml (1 tsp) fine sea salt
150ml (¼ pint) filtered water

1. Quarter and remove the stalks from the Chinese leaves, then chop into 4cm (1½in) pieces. Put in a large bowl, sprinkle over the salt, then massage the leaves with your hands for 5 minutes. You should now have a reduced volume of leaves in briny juices. Put a plate on top of the Chinese leaves and leave for 2 hours.
2. Meanwhile, peel the garlic and ginger and roughly chop. Put the pieces in a small food processor with the sugar, gochugaru and fish sauce and blend to a paste.
3. Thinly peel the mooli and cut into 2cm (¾in) matchstick strips. Trim the spring onions and cut on the diagonal into 2cm (¾in) lengths.

4 Tip the Chinese leaves into a colander and drain well, then rinse under cold running water and drain again. Taste to check the saltiness; if it is too salty, rinse and drain again.

5 Return the Chinese leaves to the bowl and add the mooli, spring onions and the spicy paste. Mix well with your hands to coat all the vegetables in the paste (use disposable plastic gloves to do this, if you prefer). Pack the vegetables into a sterilised 1 litre (1¾ pint) glass jar, packing firmly.

6 To make the brine, stir the salt and water together in a jug until the salt has dissolved. If it doesn't dissolve completely, you may need to gently heat the brine, then cool. Pour enough over the cabbage mixture to completely cover, leaving a 5cm (2in) fermenting space at the top of the jar.

7 Put on the lid, close firmly, and then loosen by a quarter turn. Leave the jar at room temperature out of direct sunlight for 5 days. 'Burp' the jar each day by opening the lid, closing firmly, then loosening by a quarter turn.

8 Taste after 5 days, then every couple of days after (up to 2 weeks), until to your liking. Store in the fridge for up to 3 months.

White Kimchi

There are many variations of kimchi and not all are made with a spice paste. This version is only mildly spiced with a seedless fresh red chilli. The Chinese leaves are soaked in a very salty brine to make them soft and supple enough to manipulate into the jar. This pickle is only fermented for a short time at room temperature, then left to mature in the fridge.

MAKES A 1 LITRE (1¾ PINT) JAR

1 head of Chinese leaves (Chinese cabbage)
100g (4oz) fine sea salt
filtered water, as needed
2 medium leeks, finely shredded
2 garlic cloves, peeled and crushed
5cm (2in) piece fresh ginger, peeled and finely grated
1 red chilli, halved and seeds removed

For the brine
15ml (1 tbsp) fine sea salt
500ml (17fl oz) filtered water

1. Quarter the Chinese leaves and remove a small amount of stalk, but leave the leaves whole and still attached in quarters. Put in a large bowl, sprinkle over the salt, pushing some between the leaves, then pour over just enough filtered water to cover. Put a plate on top of the Chinese leaves to keep them submerged and leave for 5–6 hours, until the leaves are very limp.
2. Drain the Chinese leaves, rinse in cold water, then return to the bowl. Cover with cold water and leave for a few minutes. Repeat several times, then taste a small piece; it should be pleasantly salty. If it is too salty, rinse and soak a few more times. Drain well and return to the bowl.

3. Mix together the leek, garlic and ginger and push and spread this mixture over and in-between each leaf. Push the Chinese leaves into a sterilised 1 litre (1¾ pint) glass jar, packing firmly, and add the halved red chilli, pushing a piece down each side of the jar.
4. To make the brine, stir the salt and water together in a jug until the salt has dissolved. If it doesn't dissolve completely, you may need to gently heat the brine, then cool. Pour the brine over the cabbage mixture to completely cover, leaving a 5cm (2in) fermenting space at the top of the jar. Place a weight on top so that it is submerged in the brine.
5. Put on the lid, close firmly and then loosen by a quarter turn. Leave the jar at room temperature out of direct sunlight for 8 hours or overnight, then leave in the fridge for 2 weeks. 'Burp' the jar every 3–4 days by opening the lid, closing firmly, then loosening by a quarter turn.
6. After 2 weeks the kimchi is ready to eat. To serve, slice the Chinese cabbage and serve with a spoonful or two of the brine, if liked. Store in the fridge for up to 6 weeks.

Pickled Beetroot and Turnips

This vibrant-coloured pickle, flavoured with ginger, is made with a whey starter which kick-starts the fermentation process. It will be ready to eat in just three to four days.

MAKES A 1 LITRE (1¾ PINT) JAR

4 medium beetroots, weighing about 400g (14oz) in total
2 medium turnips, weighing about 400g (14oz) in total
2.5cm (1in) piece fresh ginger
20g (¾oz) coarse crystal sea salt or sea salt flakes
200ml (7fl oz) filtered water
150ml (¼ pint) whey (page 50)

1. Thinly peel the beetroot and turnips, then cut into 5mm (¼in) thick slices. Cut the slices into 5mm (¼in) matchstick strips. Peel the ginger and slice as thinly as possible, then cut into very fine matchstick strips.
2. Put the beetroot, turnip and ginger in a bowl and mix together, then transfer to a sterilised 1 litre (1¾ pint) jar, packing as tightly as possible.
3. Stir the salt into the water until dissolved. Add about half of the salted water to the whey, then pour the mixture over the vegetables. Add enough of the remaining brine to just cover the vegetables, leaving a 5cm (2in) fermenting space at the top of the jar. If you need to, add a glass pickling weight or a clean small saucer that fits inside the jar to keep the vegetables under the liquid.
4. Put on the lid, close firmly, and then loosen by a quarter turn. Leave the jar at room temperature out of direct sunlight for 7 days. 'Burp' the jar each day by opening the lid, closing firmly, then loosening by a quarter turn.
5. Taste after 3 days, then every day after (up to 7 days), until to your liking. Store in the fridge for up to 3 months.

Carrot Kraut with Ginger and Orange

This is a delicious sweet and tangy accompaniment, packed with beta-carotene. If possible, use a food processor to grate or shred the carrots as the process is quite laborious by hand.

MAKES A 1 LITRE (1¾ PINT) JAR

25g (1oz) coarse crystal sea salt or sea salt flakes
750ml (1¼ pints) filtered water
450g (1lb) carrots, peeled and coarsely grated or shredded
2.5cm (1in) piece fresh ginger, peeled and finely grated
rind of 1 unwaxed orange
75ml (5 tbsp) whey (page 50)

1. First make a brine by gently heating the salt in a small saucepan with 150ml (¼ pint) of the water, stirring frequently until dissolved. Remove from the heat and add the rest of the water. Leave to cool.
2. Mix the carrots with the ginger and orange rind and spoon into a sterilised 1 litre (1¾ pint) jar, packing as tightly as possible.
3. Mix the whey with about half of the brine and pour over the carrot mixture. Add enough of the remaining brine to just cover the carrots, leaving a 5cm (2in) fermenting space at the top of the jar.
4. Add a glass pickling weight or a clean small saucer that fits inside the jar to keep the carrots submerged.
5. Put on the lid, close firmly, and then loosen by a quarter turn. Leave the jar at room temperature out of direct sunlight for 3 days. 'Burp' the jar each day by opening the lid, closing firmly, then loosening by a quarter turn.
6. Taste after 3 days, then every day after (up to 7 days), until to your liking. Store in the fridge for up to 2 months.

Preserved Lemons

Known as 'l'hamd mrakad' in Morocco, preserved lemons are widely used in Middle Eastern cooking to add an intense flavour to many dishes such as tagines. Only the rind, which contains the essential oils, is generally used in recipes.

MAKES A 1 LITRE (1¾ PINT) JAR

6 unwaxed lemons
fine crystal sea salt
100ml (4fl oz) fresh lemon juice
about 150ml (¼ pint) filtered water

1. Wash the lemons in cold water, then cut each into six or eight wedges (depending on the size of the lemons).
2. Press a generous amount of sea salt on to the cut surface of each lemon wedge. Pack the salted wedges tightly into a sterilised 1 litre (1¾ pint) jar. Close the jar and leave for 3 days to allow the skins to soften.
3. Open the jar and press down the lemons. Pour in the lemon juice, then top up the jar with just enough filtered water to cover the lemons, leaving a 5cm (2in) fermenting space at the top of the jar. If you need to, add a glass pickling weight or small clean saucer that fits inside the jar to keep the lemons under the liquid.
4. Put on the lid, close firmly, and then loosen by a quarter turn. Leave the jar at room temperature out of direct sunlight for 14 days. 'Burp' the jar each day by opening the lid, closing firmly, then loosening by a quarter turn. Once fermented, store in the fridge for at least 2 weeks before using.
5. To use, rinse the preserved lemons well to remove some of the salt, then pull off and discard the flesh. Cut the lemon rind into strips or leave in chunks. (The salted lemon juice can be used in various recipes such as salad dressings, marinades and sauces, but remember to reduce the amount of salt in the dish you are making.)

Probiotic Tomato Ketchup

Ketchup is a popular condiment in most households and although it's very often thought of as an accompaniment to 'junk food', it is actually good for you – tomatoes are packed with lycopene, one of the free-radical fighting antioxidants.

MAKES A 500ML (17FL OZ) BOTTLE

15ml (1 tbsp) sunflower or olive oil
1 onion, peeled and chopped
1 garlic clove, peeled and roughly chopped
1 bay leaf
45ml (3 tbsp) cider vinegar
600g (1lb 6oz) fresh ripe tomatoes, peeled (page 117) and roughly chopped or 350ml (12fl oz) passata
30ml (2 tbsp) maple syrup or dark muscovado sugar
pinch of sea salt
pinch of cayenne pepper or dried chilli flakes (optional)
10ml (2 tsp) sauerkraut juice or whey (page 50)

1. Heat the oil in a saucepan and gently fry the onion for 5 minutes, stirring frequently. Add the garlic and cook for a further 2–3 minutes or until the onion is soft.
2. Add the bay leaf and vinegar and stir for 1 minute, then add the tomatoes or passata. Bring to the boil, turn down the heat and gently bubble uncovered for 30 minutes, stirring occasionally.
3. Add the maple syrup or muscovado sugar, salt and cayenne pepper or dried chilli flakes, if using. Simmer for a further 10 minutes or until thick (it will thicken further on cooling).
4. Remove from the heat and leave to cool, then blend until smooth. Stir in the sauerkraut juice or whey and pour into a sterilised bottle or jar.
5. Put on the lid, close firmly, and then loosen by a quarter turn. Leave the jar at room temperature out of direct sunlight for 4 days. 'Burp' the jar each day by opening the lid, closing firmly, then loosening by a quarter turn. Tighten the lid and store in the fridge for up to 2 months.

Pineapple Pickle

This is a lovely, juicy, fresh-tasting pickle with just a hint of heat and colour from the chillies. Use it to spice up simple sandwiches or to accompany a cold buffet.

MAKES A 1 LITRE (1¾ PINT) JAR

1 large ripe pineapple, peeled, cored and roughly chopped
2.5cm (1in) piece fresh root ginger, peeled and chopped
2.5ml (½ tsp) fresh sea salt
1 fresh red chilli, halved, deseeded and chopped
1 fresh green chilli, halved, deseeded and chopped (optional)
60ml (4 tbsp) whey (page 50)

1. Put the pineapple, ginger and salt in a food processor and process for about 30 seconds. Add the chopped red chilli and green chilli, if using, and whey, then process again until the pineapple and chillies are chopped into fairly small pieces.
2. Transfer to a sterilised 1 litre (1¾ pint) jar, pushing down the pineapple to submerge it in the liquid and leaving a 5cm (2in) fermenting space at the top of the jar.
3. Put on the lid, close firmly, and then loosen by a quarter turn. Leave the jar at room temperature out of direct sunlight for 2 days. 'Burp' the jar each day by opening the lid, closing firmly, then loosening by a quarter turn.
4. Tighten the lid, then store the pineapple pickle in the fridge. Use within 2 months of making.

Fermented Mango Preserve

This has a sweet and slightly sour flavour and can be served as a chutney. It makes a tasty accompaniment to cold meats and Indian curries and also works well as a sweet topping for desserts such as yogurts or ice cream.

MAKES A 500ML (17FL OZ) JAR

4 ripe mangoes, peeled, stones removed and cut into 1cm (½in) chunks
50g (2oz) raisins
50g (2oz) skinned (blanched) almonds, roughly chopped
2.5cm (1in) piece fresh ginger, peeled and finely grated
10ml (2 tsp) ground cinnamon
5ml (1 tsp) fine sea salt
75ml (5 tbsp) freshly squeezed lemon juice
30ml (2 tbsp) whey (page 50)
basic brine (page 10), as needed

1. Put the chopped mangoes, raisins, almonds, ginger, cinnamon, salt and lemon juice in a bowl. Mix together, then cover with a clean tea towel or cling film and leave at room temperature for 1 hour.
2. Mix again, then pack into a sterilised 500ml (17fl oz) jar as tightly as possible. Pour in the whey, then, if needed, add enough brine to cover the mixture, leaving a 5cm (2in) fermenting space at the top of the jar.
3. Put on the lid, close firmly, and then loosen by a quarter turn. Leave the jar at room temperature out of direct sunlight for 2–4 days, or until it tastes pleasantly sour. 'Burp' the jar each day by opening the lid, closing firmly, then loosening by a quarter turn.
4. Tighten the lid, then store the mango preserve in the fridge. Use within 2 months of making.

CHAPTER 3

Fermented Dairy and Dairy Alternatives

In the Western world, we take fresh milk and dairy food for granted, but in the days before cold-storage transportation and refrigeration, dairy food had to be sourced locally and fresh milk used within a day, unless you were wealthy and fortunate enough to have an icebox, kept cool by huge blocks of ice, or a purpose-built underground icehouse. Around the world, different ways of preserving daily food were created, mostly involving fermentation. It is likely that fermented milk products were all discovered accidentally as a result of storing milk in warm climates.

Yogurt-making dates back at least as far as the third century BC and was probably first made by Turkish shepherds (the word 'yogurt' is Turkish) who carried milk in animal skins. It is likely that the bacteria from the skins reacted with the milk and formed yogurt. This food quickly spread throughout the Mediterranean and Middle East as well as Asia. Turkish migrants took their yogurt-making skills to North America in the 1700s, and it remained popular in their community. However, it wasn't enjoyed by the majority of Americans until the 1940s, when a sweetened yogurt containing fruit was marketed, and it became increasingly popular in the Western world in the 1960s and 70s.

Kefir came about in much the same way when shepherds of the Caucasus mountain region let cows' or goats' milk ferment in goatskin bags. Many myths surround kefir: the shepherds believed the grains were a gift from the prophet Mohammed, not to be shared with outsiders or their healing properties would be lost. The grains and process of making kefir were a closely guarded secret, passed from generation to generation. It was centuries before kefir production spread throughout countries surrounding the mountains, including Syria, Iraq and Iran, and in the early twentieth century to Russia, where it remains a popular health beverage.

There are many other fermented milk products, including soured cream and crème fraiche, cultured butter and buttermilk, which were traditionally made by leaving unpasteurised cream in a warm place until it had fermented thanks to the action of lactic acid bacteria. You'll find recipes for all of them in this chapter.

Yogurt

Yogurt is made by fermenting warmed pasteurised milk with lactic acid cultures. Easily digested, it's a great source of protein, calcium and B vitamins. Most yogurts on sale are 'live' (although it may not say this on the label) and contain beneficial bacteria. When yogurt is made, these bacteria consume lactose in the milk and convert them to lactic acid, giving yogurt that classic tangy taste. Lactic acid production lowers the pH of the milk, which allows it to be stored longer, and also alters the protein structure, giving yogurt its texture.

Yogurt is simple to make, cheaper than shop-bought and can be made with the milk of your choice: full fat, semi-skimmed or skimmed, depending on how rich you want your yogurt to be.

MAKES 600ML (1 PINT)

600ml (1 pint) milk
30ml (2 tbsp) plain live yogurt (see Note) or whey (page 50)

1. Pour the milk into a saucepan and heat until it reaches 82°C (180°F) on a thermometer or until it is steaming hot but not starting to boil. This destroys any bacteria in the milk that might compete with the lactic acid cultures.
2. Leave the milk to cool until it is around 37°C (98°F). If you don't have a thermometer, dip your little finger (well-washed) into the milk; you should be able to comfortably keep it there for 5 seconds.
3. Blend a little of the warm milk and yogurt together in a bowl, then stir into the rest of the milk. Pour the milk into a yogurt maker, if you have one, or a wide-neck flask, or a bowl. If using a bowl, cover and leave in a warm place such as an airing cupboard for 8–10 hours, by which time it will have thickened and set. Transfer to the fridge and use within a week of making.

Note
If you are using a shop-bought yogurt as a starter and want to check that it contains 'live' bacteria, blend 15ml (1 tbsp) yogurt with 75ml (5 tbsp) gently warmed milk in a small bowl. Leave in a warm place for at least 6 hours or overnight. If the mixture solidifies, there are live cultures present.

Variations
- For almond milk yogurt, substitute 600ml (1 pint) almond milk and use the powder from 2 probiotic capsules.
- Yogurt can be served plain or flavoured as you like. Try fresh red berries, chopped tropical fruits, dried fruits soaked in a little orange juice, nuts or unsweetened flaked coconut and simple spices such as pure vanilla extract or ground cinnamon.

Greek Yogurt and Whey

Traditionally, Greek yogurt was made from full-fat sheep's milk, but most shop-bought versions now use cows' milk. It is simply made by straining to remove some of the liquid (whey), making it rich and thick. Yogurts labelled 'Greek style' may be thickened with additives such as gelatine, so always check the label.

To make your own Greek yogurt, first follow the recipe for yogurt (page 49). Pour it into a sieve lined with muslin and suspended over a bowl. Leave in the fridge for 4–6 hours: the liquid whey will slowly drip through into the bowl, leaving a firm, thicker yogurt in the sieve. Keep the whey for making more yogurt or to use as a fermenting starter in recipes such as Dill Pickles (page 28) and Pickled Beetroot and Turnips (page 40), where it speeds up the fermentation process.

Labneh

This fresh cheese, of Middle Eastern origin, is made by draining yogurt in exactly the same way as you would when making Greek Yogurt (page 50), but is then left to drain for much longer so that it is firm enough to be rolled into small balls. It is usually rolled in olive oil and coated with fresh herbs, as here.

MAKES 500G (20OZ)

1kg (2.2 lbs) full-fat plain yogurt (page 49)
2.5ml (½ tsp) salt
15ml (1 tbsp) extra virgin olive oil
30ml (2 tbsp) chopped fresh herbs such as parsley, chives or dill

1. Place a plastic or stainless steel sieve over a bowl (make sure it will fit in your fridge) and line with a large double layer square of muslin (cheesecloth). Stir the yogurt and salt together and pour into the sieve (you may need to do this in batches, allowing the yogurt to partially drain before adding more).
2. Leave the yogurt to drain in the fridge for about 2 hours, removing the whey if it starts to touch the bottom of the sieve (keep this for drinking or use in other recipes).
3. Carefully fold the muslin in towards the centre and twist into a neat package; this will help it drain quicker. Leave in the fridge for at least 12 hours and preferably 18–24 hours; the longer you leave it, the firmer the cheese will be.
4. Roll the labneh into small walnut-sized balls and toss in a mixture of olive oil and herbs. Store in the fridge until needed and use within 3 days of making.

Coconut Yogurt

This delicious dairy alternative is made with creamed coconut (see Note) and either probiotic capsules or a powdered starter culture.

MAKES ABOUT 500ML (17FL OZ)

200g (7oz) block creamed coconut
300ml (½ pint) very hot (not boiling) filtered water
2 probiotic capsules or 2.5ml (½ tsp) powdered starter culture (for yogurts)

1. Roughly chop the creamed coconut and place in a heatproof jug. Pour over the hot water, leave to stand for a few minutes, then stir until the coconut has dissolved and the mixture is smooth.
2. Leave until the coconut mixture has cooled to around 37°C (98°F). Sprinkle over the powdered contents of the probiotic capsules or the starter culture and mix well.
3. Pour into a yogurt maker, if you have one, and follow the manufacturer's instructions. Alternatively, pour into a wide-neck flask (pour in boiling water first, leave for 3 minutes, then pour out and cool for a minute or two), or a clean sterilised jar. If using a jar, cover with a lid and leave in a warm place such as an insulated cool bag or airing cupboard.

4 Allow the yogurt to develop for 12 hours, by which time it will have thickened and set. For a slightly thicker and more tangy yogurt, leave for up to 24 hours (the longer you leave it, the more pronounced the tart flavour). Transfer to the fridge (the flavour and texture will be thicker and more yogurty after 24 hours' chilling) and use within a week of making.

Note
Sold as a solid block, creamed coconut is the unsweetened, dehydrated flesh of a mature coconut that has been ground to a smooth paste, then compressed. Not to be confused with coconut cream, which is a concentrated liquid. Creamed coconut has an intense flavour and can be stored at room temperature for several months.

Coconut Drinking Yogurt

This creamy blend has a thick pouring consistency. It can be served as a drink, used in shakes and smoothies or poured over cereals.

MAKES ABOUT 400ML (14FL OZ)

400ml (14fl oz) can full-fat coconut milk
2 probiotic capsules or 2.5ml (½ tsp) powdered starter culture (for yogurts)

1. Tip the coconut milk into a saucepan and gently heat until tepid. If the coconut milk has separated during storage (the fat often floats to the top of the can and solidifies), whisk until blended.
2. Sprinkle over the powdered contents of the probiotic capsules or the starter culture and mix well.
3. Pour into a yogurt maker, if you have one, and follow the manufacturer's instructions. Alternatively, pour into a wide-neck flask (pour in boiling water first, leave for 3 minutes, then pour out and cool for a minute or two), or a clean sterilised jar. If using a jar, cover with a lid and leave in a warm place such as an insulated cool bag or airing cupboard.
4. Allow the drinking yogurt to develop for 12–24 hours, depending on how tangy you like it, by which time it will have thickened. Transfer to the fridge, where it will thicken a little more, and use within a week of making.

> **Note**
> Save 75ml (5 tbsp) of the drinking yogurt to make the next batch, but only do this for one ferment, then make the following batch using probiotic capsules or a starter culture.

Yogurt kits

Many health-food stores and kitchen shops sell sachets of yogurt starter and these come in a huge range of types – including plain, Greek yogurt, low-fat – and flavours including a wide range of fruits, from berries to tropical as well as popular flavourings such as coconut, caramel, coffee and chocolate. Most sachets will make 1 litre (1¾ pints) yogurt and contain dried milk powder, emulsifier, sugar, flavourings and live lactic acid cultures. They are usually blended with water, but sometimes with milk. Make sure you pick one containing live cultures and try to avoid those with a very high sugar or artificial flavouring content.

Soured Cream

This is great as a topping for baked potatoes or to dollop on top of soups, tacos, nachos and desserts. You'll need to buy a pot of soured cream to start with, then save the last few spoonfuls of each batch to make the next one, or you can use live plain yogurt.

MAKES ABOUT 300ML (½ PINT)

30ml (2 tbsp) whey (page 50)
30ml (2 tbsp) organic soured cream or live plain yogurt (page 49)
300ml (½ pint) organic double cream

1. Stir the whey and soured cream or yogurt together in a bowl or jar, then stir in the double cream. Cover with muslin (cheesecloth) or a piece of tightly woven cloth, secured with an elastic band.
2. Leave at room temperature for 12–24 hours or until it has just set, like a firm wobbly yogurt. Cover with a lid or cling film and chill before using. Store in the fridge and use within 2 weeks of making.

Note
To make crème fraiche, use 30ml (2 tbsp) shop-bought cultured buttermilk instead of the soured cream or yogurt.

Cultured Butter and Buttermilk

One of the oldest ways to preserve cream was to turn it into butter. Before refrigeration, all butters were cultured, as the cream would usually have started to ferment before enough was gathered to start making butter. Cultured butter has a lovely flavour and also contains beneficial bacteria.

The basic process is to shake the cream until it separates into butter and a residual liquid known as buttermilk. Although its name may suggest otherwise, buttermilk is virtually fat-free and contains live cultures. The pale yellow clear liquid can be served as a drink, used as a starter for fermented foods such as pickled vegetables, or in cooking. It's well known as a raising agent for baked goods such as scones and is often added to meat marinades where its microbes and mild acidity act as a tenderiser. This old-style buttermilk is rarely found in the shops and when it is, will usually be labelled 'traditional buttermilk'. Most commercial buttermilk is a cultured milk product made in a similar way to yogurt. It is a milky colour rather than clear and can be used in the same way as traditional buttermilk.

MAKES ABOUT 225G (8OZ) BUTTER AND 225ML (8FL OZ) BUTTERMILK

600ml (1 pint) cultured double cream, e.g. full-fat crème fraiche (page 56 and see Note)
150ml (¼ pint) iced water
fine sea salt (optional)

1. Pour the cream into a chilled bowl and, using an electric whisk, whip the cream at a low speed until it thickens. You can also do this in a blender or a food processor fitted with a metal blade or by shaking by hand in a jar.
2. Continue whisking until the cream has solidified into butter and liquid forms in the bowl. Tip into a plastic sieve over a jug or bowl and let it drain; keep the liquid as this is the buttermilk and will store in the fridge for up to a week in a clean bottle or jar.

FERMENTED DAIRY AND DAIRY ALTERNATIVES

3 Tip the butter back into the bowl and pour over the iced water. Stir and press with a wooden spoon to extract any remaining buttermilk. Tip into the sieve and let it drain again. Discard this liquid as it will be very diluted buttermilk.
4 If you like, put the butter in a double layer of muslin (cheesecloth) and squeeze out the last few drops of liquid. Return to the bowl and beat in the salt, if using.
5 Put the butter in a bowl and cover with cling film or in an airtight container; you can shape it into a block first if you like. It will keep in the fridge for 3–4 weeks.

Note
When making cultured cream or crème fraiche for butter, reduce the fermentation time, so that it is only partially fermented.

MILK KEFIR GRAINS VERSUS POWDERED KEFIR STARTER CULTURES

Which is easiest to use?

Both milk kefir grains and powdered starter cultures are easy to use, but of the two, powdered starter culture is simpler for first-time kefir-makers, produces consistent results and also suits those who do not want to make kefir regularly.

Which is more versatile?

A powdered kefir starter culture can be used for dairy milk, coconut milk, coconut water or fruit juice, whereas milk kefir grains can only be used to culture dairy milk or coconut milk. Other non-dairy milks such as soya and nut milks can be cultured using milk kefir grains, but the results are inconsistent and the kefir rarely thickens.

Which is more economical?

Milk kefir grains are initially more expensive to buy than powdered starter cultures, but can work out much cheaper in the long run as they should last indefinitely. Because they multiply and grow over time, you may find a friend or neighbour who is willing to give you a spoonful of milk kefir grains to start your own colony. Powdered starter cultures are 'single use' cultures, i.e. they are meant to be used only once, although with care they can be re-cultured several times before the bacterial culture weakens.

Which is healthier?

Generally, powdered kefir starter culture has seven to nine strains of beneficial bacteria, whereas milk kefir grains (and water kefir grains) have many more, as well as numerous yeast species.

TIPS FOR MAKING KEFIR FROM MILK KEFIR GRAINS

When your grains first arrive, you may be surprised by the tiny amount you've received. It should be just enough to make your first batch. You will find that with each batch, the grains will grow and multiply and you will soon have a larger amount. You can then divide the batch and use to make more kefir or give a portion of the grains to friends and family.

Sometimes it takes the grains a while to settle into a 'new home' and your first batch of kefir may taste a bit more 'yeasty' than the ready-made kefir you can buy in the shops. This is still perfectly good to drink and you'll find the kefir grains will settle and the flavour will mellow after just a few batches.

However, generally, it is best to make the first batch with less milk: around 250ml (8fl oz) is enough for the small amount of kefir grains you will have. Depending on the flavour of the first batch, you may choose to discard it and start a second batch with the revived milk kefir grains. Build up the amount of milk you use gradually: 350ml (12fl oz) for the second batch and 450ml (¾ pint) for the third. From then on, you can use the full amount of milk given in the recipe.

Fermentation time can vary greatly: on a very warm day, 10–12 hours may be plenty. The longer you ferment, the more acidic your kefir will be and the lower it will be in lactose.

The milk you use for culturing will determine the taste and texture of the finished kefir. The grains thrive best in full-fat milk, but you can use semi-skimmed or skimmed milk if you prefer, although the results will be thinner. Cows' milk is the most popular choice and produces a thick and creamy kefir. Goats' milk kefir tends to be thinner. It is naturally homogenised, so the cream will not separate as much during culturing. If you want to make goats' milk kefir, you can buy grains specifically for this which have been previously cultured in goats' milk. Sheep's milk contains more protein than cows' milk, so produces a thicker, creamier kefir; it also has a sweeter flavour.

Raw milk can also be used (in which case do not heat as in step 1), but it is not advised and you should be aware of the health risks of using unpasteurised milk. If you do decide to use raw milk, make sure it is really fresh and was chilled quickly, as any bacterial content (which would be destroyed by pasteurisation) may compete with the bacteria in milk kefir grains and impede the fermentation process. Lactose-free milk is generally unsuitable for culturing as it is usually filtered to remove lactose, which is needed to 'feed' the beneficial bacteria. At the end of culturing, kefir is very low in lactose and often suits those who have a mild to moderate dairy intolerance; the longer you allow it to ferment, the lower the lactose content.

Kefir has a slightly tart flavour with no hint of sweetness, so you may wish to flavour with a little honey, agave or maple syrup or blend with a little ripe fresh fruit when serving.

Caring for your kefir grains

- Remember that your kefir grains are a living organism. Keep them away from heat and out of direct sunlight. If you have a sunny kitchen, putting the jar in a cardboard box on the work surface is a good idea, as it's easily forgotten if you store it in a cupboard.
- Never use metal sieves or spoons when making; plastic or wooden spoons (keep one specifically for kefir-making) and a nylon sieve are essential.
- If your kefir grains start to smell odd, or you think they may have died, don't throw them away. Rinse with filtered (non-chlorinated) water, put in a glass bowl with filtered water and store in the fridge for 24 hours. Strain, then test by making a small batch of kefir.
- If you don't want to start another batch of kefir straight away, store the kefir grains in a small jar or bowl of whole milk, covered with a tight-fitting lid or cling film, in the fridge, where the low temperature will slow down the fermentation process, keeping them in a semi-dormant state. Change the milk after a week (it will have made a small amount of kefir, which you can drink). If you need to leave for longer than a week, leave the grains in a little more milk, then strain off the milk and discard and rinse the grains in filtered water before making a batch of kefir.

FERMENTED DAIRY AND DAIRY ALTERNATIVES

Milk Kefir

A close relative of yogurt, although much thinner in consistency, kefir is a fermented milk drink, bursting with billions of probiotics. It can be made using a powdered starter or with kefir grains, which you can purchase in health-food stores or on the internet. After making a batch of kefir, the grains are strained out and can be used to create the next batch.

MAKES 900ML (1½ PINTS)

900ml (1½ pints) organic whole milk
1 packet kefir starter or 30ml (2 tbsp) milk kefir grains

1. Pour the milk into a saucepan and put over a medium heat until it reaches 82°C (180°F) on a thermometer. This will ensure there are no other microbes in the milk, although some consider heating the milk unnecessary, as microbes in the kefir should quickly dominate any other microbes present.
2. Let the milk cool to 40°C (110°F) or warm it to this temperature if you are using milk straight from the fridge.
3. Pour the milk into a 1 litre (1¾ pint) jar and add the kefir starter or grains. Put on the lid and gently shake, then loosen the lid by a quarter turn. Or cover the jar with a double layer of muslin or a clean piece of cloth, held securely with an elastic band.
4. Leave at room temperature, out of direct light, for 24–48 hours (the time will depend on how warm your room is). Give the jar a gentle shake a couple times if possible to ensure all the milk is fermenting (if you've used a lid, remember to tighten before shaking, then loosen again).

5 Give the jar a final shake. If you've used milk kefir grains, strain the kefir through a plastic or stainless steel sieve into a clean jar. Store the kefir in the fridge; it should keep well for 2–3 weeks, but if it starts to smell yeasty or taste unpleasantly sour, it should be discarded.
6 Rinse the kefir grains in filtered water, then start the kefir-making process again (or see 'Caring for your kefir grains', page 61). If you used a packet of kefir starter, reserve 150ml (¼ pint) kefir to make the next batch.

Note
Home-made milk kefir may be thinner than shop-bought kefir and will have the consistency of single cream.

Coconut Milk Kefir

Either kefir milk grains or powdered kefir starter can be used to make coconut milk kefir. If using kefir milk grains, you will need to 'revitalise' the kefir grains (see steps 4 to 6) between batches.

MAKES 800ML (1 PINT 7FL OZ)

2 x 400ml (14fl oz) cans full-fat coconut milk
1 packet kefir starter or 30ml (2 tbsp) milk kefir grains

1. Shake the cans well to mix the coconut milk, then pour into a 1 litre (1¾ pint) jar and add the kefir starter or grains. Put on the lid and gently shake, then loosen the lid by quarter turn. Or cover the jar with a double layer of muslin or a clean piece of cloth, held securely with an elastic band.
2. Leave at room temperature, out of direct light, for 24 hours (the time will depend on how warm your room is). Give the jar a gentle shake a couple times if possible to ensure all the milk is fermenting (if you've used a lid, remember to tighten before shaking, then loosen again afterwards).
3. Give the jar a final shake, then strain the coconut kefir through a plastic or stainless steel sieve into a clean jar. Store the kefir in the fridge; it should keep well for 2–3 weeks, but if it starts to smell yeasty or taste unpleasantly sour, it should be discarded.

4 If you have used milk kefir grains, you will need to revitalise them before making another batch of coconut milk kefir or dairy milk kefir. Rinse the kefir grains in filtered water, then place them in a small jar, adding 100ml (4fl oz) whole dairy milk.
5 Put on the lid and gently shake, then loosen the lid by a quarter turn. Or cover the jar with a double layer of muslin or a clean piece of cloth, held securely with an elastic band. Leave at room temperature, out of direct light, for 24 hours.
6 Drain the dairy-milk kefir (you can drink this if you like, but it will only be lightly cultured as the kefir grains take a while to revitalise), then gently rinse the grains in filtered water if using to make more coconut milk kefir. You do not need to rinse the grains if making dairy milk kefir.

Kefir Soft Cheese

Making kefir cheese is easy and it contains all the beneficial bacteria of kefir in a concentrated form. This silky soft cheese is similar in texture to cream cheese, but slightly more spreadable and less rich, with a distinctive tart kefir flavour. Leave plain or flavour with chopped fresh herbs and spread on Sourdough (page 84) or crackers. It's delicious topped with some fermented vegetables such as kimchi or with fine slices of smoked salmon.

MAKES 300-350G (11-12OZ)

1 litre (1¾ pints) Milk Kefir (page 62) or Coconut Milk Kefir (page 64)
1.5ml (¼ tsp) fine sea salt (optional)

1. Make the kefir, allowing it to ferment for about 48 hours; it should be very thick and the curds and whey may be starting to separate out. The time this takes will depend on the temperature of the room; it will take less time in warm weather.
2. Line a large plastic or stainless steel sieve with a double layer of muslin (cheesecloth) or use a nut bag, and place over a bowl.
3. Carefully pour the kefir into the muslin, cover the bowl with cling film and leave in the fridge for an hour or two. The whey will slowly drip into the bowl (you can drink this or use it in cooking). Drain off the first batch of whey (or it may rise above the base of the sieve), then return to the fridge and leave to drip for a further 12-24 hours.
4. Tip the cheese into a bowl and stir in the salt, if using. Keep the cheese in a covered container in the fridge for up to 2 weeks.

Note
The longer you leave the kefir cheese to drip, the thicker the cheese (and the less cheese you will end up with), so check occasionally until it is the desired thickness.

Kefir Cream

Made in the same way as kefir, but with cream rather than milk. Choose an organic cream if available, making sure it is well within its use-by date. The higher the fat content of the cream, the thicker your kefir cream will be. Similar in flavour to soured cream, kefir cream can be used in exactly the same way.

MAKES ABOUT 300ML (½ PINT)

300ml (½ pint) double cream, preferably organic
10ml (2 tsp) milk kefir grains

1. Pour the cream into a very clean bowl or sterilised jar, then gently stir in the kefir grains. Cover the jar with a double layer of muslin (cheesecloth) or cloth secured with an elastic band, or a loose lid.
2. Leave at room temperature for 12–24 hours, until it has just set, like a firm yogurt. Scoop out the kefir grains with a fine plastic slotted spoon.
3. If you're not using the kefir grains again straight away, rinse in cold filtered water, then store in a small jar of whole fresh milk in the fridge for up to 10 days.
4. Cover the kefir cream with a lid or cling film and chill before serving. It will keep in the fridge for up to 2 weeks.

> **Note**
> Do not allow the cream to get too thick or it will be difficult to scoop out the kefir grains. If you want a very thick cream, use 30ml (2 tbsp) cultured milk kefir instead of the kefir grains.

CHAPTER 4

Fermented Drinks

One of the simplest ways to ensure you get a daily helping of beneficial bacteria is to have a small glass of fermented drink. Here, you'll find a wide selection to suit all tastes, from kombucha and rejuvelac to sparkling orange juice and water kefir. Many of these drinks are not only good for your gut, but are packed with vitamins, too.

You will need to buy water kefir grains or a kombucha starter from a health-food store or via the Internet, but once you have them you can keep them healthy and active for many months.

Water Kefir

This makes an excellent dairy-free alternative to milk kefir. It tastes like a dry (rather than sweet), slightly fizzy lemonade and has a faintly fermented flavour. Sometimes called 'tibicos', 'tibi' or 'Japanese water crystals', water kefir is rich in beneficial bacteria and micronutrients. The crystal-like grains, which may be clear or golden brown, are cultured in sugar water. This isn't, as it may first sound, unhealthy: after fermentation, water kefir becomes a relatively low-sugar, low-calorie drink, as the sugar and fruit feed the kefir grains and most of the sugar is converted to acetic acid in the process.

MAKES 900ML (1½ PINTS)

900ml (1½ pints) filtered water
65g (2½oz) sugar, preferably organic
25g (1oz) organic raisins or other unsulphured dried fruit,
　e.g. figs, or 1.5ml (¼ tsp) molasses
½ unwaxed organic lemon (optional)
2 slices fresh ginger, peeled (optional)
5g (¼oz) sachet of water kefir grains

1 Put the water in a sterilised 1 litre (1¾ pint) glass jar or jug. Add the sugar and molasses, if using, and stir until dissolved, then add the raisins or dried fruit, lemon and ginger, if using.
2 Add the water kefir grains and cover the top of the jar or jug with muslin (cheesecloth), held in place with an elastic band. Alternatively, put a lid on the jar, then loosen by a quarter turn to allow some of the fermenting gases to escape.
3 Leave the jar at room temperature away from direct sunlight for 24–36 hours, depending on the strength you prefer.
4 Strain the kefir through a nylon sieve and discard the raisins, ginger and lemon. Serve straight away with ice, or bottle and store in the fridge. Reserve the kefir grains to start another batch (or store in the fridge in sugared water for up to 10 days). See Notes.

Notes
- Don't be tempted to use honey instead of sugar when making water kefir, as it has anti-microbial properties which will slow the growth of the grains.
- You can use other unsulphured dried fruit when making water kefir, such as apricots or cherries; the latter will give the kefir a pretty pale pink colour.
- As well as live fresh grains, you can buy dehydrated kefir grains. These are dormant and can be stored in a dry cool place for up to a year (make sure you buy freshly dehydrated grains for the maximum shelf life). Dried grains can take a while to be fully active, so you may need to discard the first ferment or two.
- You can also buy ginger water kefir crystals, which are grown in a mixture containing both fresh root and powdered ginger. They produce a ginger-ale like version of water kefir.
- When storing water kefir in bottles, keep refrigerated (for up to a week) to slow down fermentation, and loosen then re-tighten the lids every couple of days to allow some of the gases to escape.
- If you don't want to make another batch of Water Kefir straight away, mix together 300ml (½ pint) filtered water and 25g (1oz) sugar until dissolved. Add the water kefir grains, cover and store in the fridge for up to 10 days. Strain as before (you should be able to drink the small amount of water kefir as storing in the fridge will have slowed down the fermentation process), then use the grains to start a fresh batch.

Coconut Water Kefir

Many health claims are made about coconut water: that it rehydrates the body quickly after sport, helps create a strong immune system and may even promote weight loss. It certainly makes a delicious-flavoured water kefir. Some brands of coconut water have a small amount of sugar added (check the ingredients label) and these are preferable for making kefir as the grains feed on sugar. If using unsweetened coconut water, stir in 5ml (1tsp) sugar until dissolved before adding the water kefir grains. Make sure your grains have been culturing in sugar water kefir for at least three weeks before making coconut water kefir. You can then make another batch.

MAKES 1 LITRE (1¾ PINTS)

1 litre (1¾ pints) coconut water
45ml (3 tbsp) hydrated water kefir grains

1. Pour the coconut water into a sterilised 1 litre (1¾ pint) glass jar or jug. Add the water kefir grains and cover the top of the jar or jug with muslin, held in place with an elastic band. Alternatively, put a lid on the jar, then loosen by a quarter turn to allow some of the fermenting gases to escape.
2. Leave the jar at room temperature away from direct sunlight for 24–36 hours, depending on the strength you like.
3. Strain the kefir through a nylon sieve. Serve straight away with ice, or bottle and store in the fridge (see storage note on page 71). Reserve the kefir grains and make a batch of Water Kefir (page 70) to feed and rejuvenate the grains. You can then make another batch of coconut water kefir.

Kombucha

This refreshing, fizzy, slightly sour drink is made from a sugary weak tea which is then fermented with the help of a 'SCOBY' (Symbiotic Culture Of Bacteria and Yeast), which may also be called the 'mother' or 'tea mushroom'. The scoby is a creamy-white jelly-like piece of cellulose that usually floats and grows on top of the kombucha, protecting the fermenting tea from the air by sealing it in its own micro-environment. Don't worry about the large amount of sugar in the recipe; most or all of it gets metabolised by the scoby, making kombucha relatively low in calories. Although it contains a very small amount of alcohol as a by-product of the fermentation process, this is usually no more than 1 per cent.

MAKES ABOUT 2 LITRES (3½ PINTS)

1.75 litres (3 pints) filtered water
125g (4½oz) white or brown sugar, preferably organic
10ml (2 tsp) loose, plain black, oolong or green tea, or 2–3 tea bags
175ml (6fl oz) kombucha starter (shop-bought or from a previous batch)
1 piece kombucha scoby, at least 7.5cm (3in) in diameter

1. Bring the water to the boil in a saucepan, remove from the heat and stir in the sugar until dissolved. Add the loose tea or tea bags and leave to steep until the liquid is cool (speed up this process if you like by placing the pan in a bowl of cold or iced water, but let the tea brew for at least 5 minutes before you do this).
2. Strain the cooled tea into a 2.25 litre (4 pint) sterilised jar, add most of the kombucha starter and stir to blend. Add the scoby (it usually floats but sometimes sinks, which is fine), then pour in the rest of the kombucha starter.

3 Cover the jar with a piece of clean, tightly woven cloth or good-quality paper towels and secure with an elastic band. Carefully move it to a warm place, out of direct sunlight, and leave undisturbed for 5–6 days. After a few days, you should see a new layer of scoby forming on the surface of the kombucha. It usually attaches to the old scoby, but it's not a problem if it doesn't. You may also see a few bubbles, brown filaments floating beneath the scoby and some sediment at the bottom of the jar; all these are signs of healthy fermentation.

4 After 6 days, taste the kombucha daily. It should be tart but not unpleasantly sour, so if it is still quite sweet, ferment a little longer, up to 10 days, checking the flavour daily.

5 When your kombucha is ready, start making the next batch in exactly the same way. With very clean hands, carefully remove the scoby and 175ml (6fl oz) of the kombucha, then strain the rest into sterilised bottles, using a funnel, leaving at least 2cm (¾in) headroom in each.

6 Put the lids on the bottles, tighten, then loosen by a quarter turn (this will allow a small amount of gas to escape). Store the bottled kombucha at room temperature and out of direct sunlight for a day to allow the kombucha to carbonate. Tighten the lids and refrigerate. Drink within 10 days of making. Release excess gas occasionally by partially unscrewing the tops, letting some of the gas escape, then tightening the tops again.

Note
Kombucha is recognised as being a detoxification aid as it contains glucuronic acid, a compound that binds with toxins and removes them from the body. It also has immune-boosting antioxidants.

TIPS AND TROUBLESHOOTING WHEN MAKING KOMBUCHA

- **Avoid metal** It's fine to briefly use metal utensils when making kombucha, e.g. for stirring, but avoid prolonged contact with metal when fermenting and storing, especially aluminium as this will give kombucha a metallic aftertaste and will weaken the scoby.
- **Flavours** Black tea will make the most successful kombucha, but green tea or oolong (or a blend) will also work well. You can use herbal teas but should combine them with at least 5ml (1 tsp) or 1 tea bag of black tea. Avoid teas that contain oils, e.g. Earl Grey, which contains bergamot, or spiced teas such as ginger, which are anti-microbial and may prevent the scoby from developing properly.
- **Taking a break** If you want to stop making kombucha for a while, or will be away for two weeks or less, make a fresh batch and leave it in a cool place out of direct sunlight. Although it will be too sour to drink after that time, it will keep the scoby alive, ready to make a fresh batch. If you need to keep for longer and up to six weeks, store the scoby in a batch of the tea in the fridge. Again, discard the kombucha and start a new batch from scratch.
- **Making more** You can increase or decrease the amount of kombucha you make, but keep the ratio of sugar, tea and liquid the same. One scoby will ferment any batch size, although larger batches may take longer to ferment, and smaller ones slightly less time.
- **Breathing space** Leave a small space between the scoby-topped tea and the top of your brewing jar, about 5cm (2in), to give the new developing scoby space to grow.
- **Keep it clean** Never clean your brewing jar with anti-bacterial washing-up liquid or soap as this may discourage the scoby from growing. Periodically, use distilled vinegar to clean your equipment.
- **Discoloured scoby** Your scoby should look like a flat pancake, be no more than 2cm (¾in) thick, and be a creamy-white colour with a few trailing brown strings. If it doesn't fit this description, don't worry. It may float on the bottom or sideways, develop lumps and bumps, clear or brown dry patches or a hole or two. All of these are fine and are just the scoby reacting to changes in its environment: it should readjust after a batch or two.

FERMENTED DRINKS

- **Aroma** Your scoby should have a fairly neutral aroma, then start to smell more sour and vinegary as the kombucha ferments. If it smells cheese-like or very unpleasant you should discard the batch of kombucha and begin again with fresh tea.
- **Keeping your scoby healthy** A scoby should last for many months; to keep it healthy, stick to the ratios of sugar, tea, starter tea and water. A younger scoby will ferment better than an older one, so every few batches, peel off the bottom oldest layer. Store the older scoby in the fridge as a back-up or give to friends to make their own kombucha. If there are signs of mould on the scoby, you should discard it and start with a new one.

Rejuvelac

Rejuvelac is a probiotic drink made by fermenting freshly sprouted wheat berries in water. It has a slightly tart lemony flavour and a subtle sweetness and contains all the goodness of the grains. It is extremely high in B vitamins and also contains vitamins E and K as well as a number of healthy enzymes. Believed to have Baltic origins, rejuvelac is closely related to the traditional Romanian drink 'bors', made from fermented wheat bran, which is used to make a sour-tasting soup known as 'ciorba'.

MAKES ABOUT 1 LITRE (1¾ PINTS)

100g (4oz) wheat berries (wheat grain), preferably organic
1 litre (1¾ pints) filtered water
5ml (1 tsp) apple cider vinegar

1 Wash the wheat berries thoroughly in cold running water, removing any that are discoloured or broken. Place the grains in a 1 litre (1¾ pint) jar and fill the jar with lukewarm water. Cover with a piece of muslin (cheesecloth) and secure with an elastic band. Leave in a warm room for 8 hours or overnight.
2 Pour out the water through the muslin, then replace with fresh water. Gently shake the jar to wash the grains, then pour out the water through the muslin. Make sure they are thoroughly drained or the grains may become rancid or mouldy. Repeat this procedure at least twice and preferably three times a day. After rinsing, leave the jar on its side in a warm place away from direct sunlight. After 2–3 days the grains should have sprouted. Keep rinsing and draining until the sprouts are about 1cm (just under ½in long).
3 Tip out the sprouted grains into a bowl, rinse one last time and drain in a sieve, removing any that haven't sprouted. Tip the sprouted grains back into the jar and add the filtered water and apple cider vinegar. Cover the jar with a piece of tightly woven cloth, secured with an elastic band (to keep out any fruit flies).

FERMENTED DRINKS

4 Leave the jar in a warm place out of direct sunlight for 2–3 days. You should see a small amount of bubbling. The rejuvelac is ready when it is cloudy and smells pleasantly sour. Pour the rejuvelac through a sieve into a large jug and serve straight away. To keep the rejuvelac for longer, pour into sealed jars or bottles and store in the fridge for up to 2 weeks. Release excess gas by unscrewing the tops a little, then tightening again daily.

Notes
- Rejuvelac is a digestive aid best consumed in small amounts first thing in the morning or between meals on an empty stomach. It can be used as a gentle natural laxative.
- Wheat berries are whole wheat grains with the husks removed; they can be bought in health-food shops and online.
- If you want to grow your own wheatgrass, soak double the quantity of wheat berries, then scatter half over a seed tray with a 2.5cm (1in) layer of moist compost. Top the wheat berries with a further 2cm (¾in) of compost. Water lightly every day, keeping the tray covered with moist newspaper. After 3 days, the wheatgrass should be about 5cm (2in) tall and yellow. Remove the newspaper and leave the tray in a light place, but out of direct sunlight, for 4–5 days; it should then be about 15–18cm (6–7in) tall and bright green in colour. Cut the wheatgrass with kitchen scissors and use in juices and smoothies.

Variations
Traditionally, rejuvelac is made with wheat berries, but it can also be made using whole rye, barley, buckwheat grains, millet or quinoa, which all have their own unique flavour.

Beetroot Kvass

With its earthy and briny flavour, kvass is a traditional Russian beverage made by fermenting beetroot or sometimes more economically with scraps of rye or wheat bread. Some versions are flavoured with wild berries, dried fruit and spices. It is often served as a digestif poured over ice and diluted with a little water, or added to recipes such as Borscht (beetroot soup, page 102) or Marinated Herring and Beetroot Salad (page 110).

MAKES ABOUT 1 LITRE (1¾ PINTS)

2 medium beetroots
30ml (2 tbsp) whey (page 50) or briny juice from previously fermented vegetables such as sauerkraut or kimchi
10ml (2 tsp) sea salt
100ml (4fl oz) filtered water, plus extra for topping up

1 Slice the top and root end off the beetroot, peel, then cut into 1cm (½in) cubes. Place in a 1 litre (1¾ pint) sterilised jar.
2 Whisk together the whey, salt and 100ml (4fl oz) filtered water in a jug until the salt has dissolved. Pour over the beetroot. Pour in enough filtered water to come within 5cm (2in) from the top of the jar.
3 Cover the top of the jar with muslin, held in place with an elastic band. Alternatively, put a lid on the jar, then loosen by a quarter turn to allow some of the fermenting gases to escape.
4 Leave the jar at room temperature away from direct sunlight for a week, then strain through a nylon sieve into a jug. Pour into a sterilised bottle and keep in the fridge. Use within 2 weeks of making.

Note
The beetroot cubes can be used in cooking (but remember they will have a salty and slightly vinegary flavour) or in a salad such as Marinated Herring and Beetroot Salad (page 110).

Sparkling Orange Juice

This fizzy and subtly sweet fermented juice is packed with good bacteria, enzymes and vitamin C. It can be made with freshly squeezed juice or you can use a carton of good-quality orange juice, but make sure it has no added sugar and is labelled 'juice' and not 'drink'.

MAKES ABOUT 900ML (1½ PINTS)

600ml (1 pint) orange juice, preferably organic
250ml (8fl oz) filtered water
30ml (2 tbsp) whey (page 50) or 2.5ml (½ tsp) powdered starter culture (for yogurts)

1. Stir together the orange juice, water and whey or starter culture in a large jug. Pour into a sterilised 1 litre (1¾ pint) jar with a screw-top lid or airlock.
2. If using a jar without an airlock, put on the lid, then loosen by a quarter turn to allow some of the fermenting gases to escape. Leave the jar at room temperature away from direct sunlight for 48 hours.
3. Transfer the jar to the fridge (tighten the lid a little, but not completely if you are using a screw-top lid) and chill well before serving. Release excess gas occasionally by unscrewing the top, then tightening again. Use within 2 weeks of making.

Variations
- For a sparkling mixed citrus drink, substitute some freshly squeezed or carton pink grapefruit and/or tangerine juice for the same quantity of orange juice.
- You can also make sparkling apple juice in exactly the same way, substituting apple juice for the orange juice.

Probiotic Limeade

This refreshing citrus drink contains both fresh lemon and lime juice. As this would be very tart, it is sweetened a little with whole cane sugar (Sucanat), but some of this is used by the beneficial bacteria during fermentation, so this is not an overly sweet or calorific drink.

MAKES ABOUT 1 LITRE (1¾ PINTS)

50g (2oz) whole cane sugar (Sucanat)
750ml (1¼ pints) filtered water
freshly squeezed juice of 3 limes
freshly squeezed juice of 1 lemon
75ml (5 tbsp) whey (page 50)

1 Put the sugar in a heavy-based saucepan and add about 300ml (½ pint) of the water. Heat gently, stirring occasionally until the sugar has dissolved. Remove from the heat and stir in most of the remaining water. Leave to cool.
2 Stir in the lime and lemon juice and the whey. Pour into a sterilised 1 litre (1¾ pint) jar with a screw-top lid or airlock. Top up with enough of the remaining water to come no higher than 2.5cm (1in) of the rim (the amount of liquid may vary depending on the size and juiciness of the citrus fruit).
3 If using a jar without an airlock, put on the lid, then loosen by a quarter turn to allow some of the fermenting gases to escape. Leave the jar at room temperature away from direct sunlight for 48 hours.
4 Transfer the jar to the fridge (tighten the lid a little, but not completely if you are using a screw-top lid) and chill well before serving. Release excess gas occasionally by unscrewing the top, then tightening again. Use within 2 weeks of making.

Note
Sucanat is essentially pure dried sugar cane juice. Unlike brown sugar, it retains its molasses content, vitamins and minerals. It can be bought in health-food stores and via the internet.

CHAPTER 5

Fermented Breads

For the earliest breads, the process of fermentation was always used for rising, and traditional bread-making sometimes took several days. Fermentation generates bubbles of carbon dioxide, which is responsible for the rise of the dough, and lactic acid. The microbes do not survive the high temperatures needed to bake the bread, but the wonderful flavour they create remains.

Sourdough Loaf

A traditional sourdough starter is made with a flour and water paste that is left to ferment naturally by wild, airborne yeast and natural yeasts in the flour. It can be a hit and miss affair, with the occasional failure, as wild yeast needs more coaxing than commercial yeast and it takes many days to create a sourdough loaf from scratch. However, the long slow development is well worth the wait and effort; it gives the bread a complex flavour and creates a crispy crust and a soft, slightly chewy interior.

The distinctive sour flavour comes from two kinds of friendly bacteria: lactobacillus and acetobacillus, which grow alongside the wild yeast and help ferment the sugars in the dough into lactic acid. It's important to use organic stoneground strong white flour, as ordinary bread flour may undergo processing that destroys any natural yeasts.

MAKES 1 LOAF

For the starter and pre-ferment
about 150g (5oz) organic stoneground strong white bread flour
filtered water

For the sourdough loaf
500g (18oz) organic stoneground strong white flour, plus extra for dusting
15g (½oz) fine sea salt
300ml (½ pint) warm filtered water

- **Day 1:** Make the starter. Mix 10ml (2 tsp) of the flour and 15ml (1 tbsp) cold filtered water in a clean wide jar. When the batter is blended and smooth, whisk it with a fork for a minute or two to help incorporate some airborne yeast to get the starter going. Leave the jar open in a warm place for about 24 hours.

- **Days 2, 3, 4 and 5:** Add 10ml (2 tsp) of the flour and 15ml (1 tbsp) cold filtered water to the jar, stirring until smooth, then cover with a clean tea towel and leave overnight. After a few days, you should notice an increasing number of bubbles on the surface. If there are no signs of life after 5 days, or if the starter smells unpleasant, throw it away and start again. Don't worry if your starter separates into a darkish liquid on top of a thicker paler paste; just stir together.
- **Day 6:** Make a 'pre-ferment' to add extra flavour and to make the airborne yeast more active. Weigh out 10g (a little less than ½oz) of the starter into a mixing bowl, then add 100g (4oz) of the flour and 100ml (4fl oz) warm filtered water. Stir well, cover with cling film and leave in a warm room for 8 hours or overnight. Store the rest of the starter in the fridge for up to a week. When you are ready to make another loaf, leave at room temperature for a few hours, then 'feed' again with 10ml (2 tsp) of flour and 15ml (1 tbsp) cold filtered water for 5 days, then make another pre-ferment from the mixture to make another loaf (or make Sourdough Pancakes, page 141).
- **Day 7**: Plan to start making the bread either early in the morning or complete the first proving just before you go to bed, as the whole proving and baking process takes at least 10 hours.

1 To make the sourdough loaf, put the flour and salt in a large bowl or in a table-top mixer fitted with a dough hook (or use the dough setting in a bread-making machine). Add the pre-ferment and water and stir with a wooden spoon, or use the slow setting in a mixer, until combined. The consistency of the pre-ferment varies from batch to batch, so add a little more flour or more water if needed, to make a soft dough.

2 If mixing by hand, turn out the dough and gently knead, stretching and folding the dough for 7–8 minutes until elastic. In a machine, mix for 4–5 minutes. Place the dough in a large, oiled bowl and cover with cling film. Leave to rise in a warm place for 3 hours. Sourdough takes much longer to rise than conventional yeasted bread, so you may see very little rise at this time.

3 Line a medium-sized bowl with a clean tea towel and dust with flour, or use a proving basket if you have one. Knead the dough again for a minute or two, then shape into a round and lightly dust with flour. Place in the bowl or basket, cover with oiled cling film and leave in a warm place for 6–8 hours (or overnight in a cool place) until doubled in size.
4 Put a large baking tray in the oven and preheat the oven to 220°C (fan 200°C), gas 7. Half fill a small roasting tin with hot water and place in the bottom of the oven to create steam during cooking.
5 Remove the baking tray from the oven and dust with flour. Carefully tip the risen dough on to the tray. Slash the top a few times with a sharp knife, then bake for 30–35 minutes until golden brown and hollow sounding when the base is tapped. Cool on a wire rack and serve warm or cold.

Variations
- For a softer crust substitute some or all of the water with milk.
- Replace half the white flour with an equal amount of organic stoneground wholemeal bread flour. This will make a loaf with a denser texture but not too heavy. You can use all stoneground wholemeal bread flour (add an extra 15ml (1 tbsp) water as well), but the loaf will be fairly heavy and dense.
- You can replace up to a quarter of the white flour with rye flour, spelt or Kamut for a more nutty flavoured loaf.

Easy Sourdough Starter

Rather than relying entirely on airborne bacteria, sourdough can also be made using commercial yeast to activate the starter. The delicious 'sour' flavour will still be provided by the action of 'friendly' bacteria. The loaf can either be oven-baked or cooked in a bread-making machine.

> 250g (9oz) organic stoneground strong white bread flour
> 10ml (2 tsp) fast-action dried yeast
> 300ml (½ pint) cold filtered water

1. Put the flour and yeast in a large bowl and stir together. Make a hollow in the middle and add the water. Gradually blend in with a wooden spoon or whisk to make a thick batter.
2. Cover with a clean tea towel and leave undisturbed in a cool room, away from direct sunlight, for 3–5 days to ferment. The batter is ready when it is frothy and has a pleasantly sour smell. Cover the bowl with cling film and store in the fridge for up to a week, or until ready to use.
3. Before using the starter, remove from the fridge and leave for about 30 minutes to reach room temperature. Stir the batter, then remove the amount required with a ladle.
4. Replenish the starter by the amount you have removed (you need to do this at least every 2 weeks). For example, if you have used 300ml (½ pint), you will need to add 150g (5oz) flour and 150ml (¼ pint) water. Let this ferment at room temperature as before, for 24 hours, then store in the fridge.

California Sourdough

The city of San Francisco is located midway along the coast of California. During the gold rush in the mid-nineteenth century, prospectors often carried a mixture of flour and water in packets strapped to their belts. Their body heat fermented the mixture to make natural leaven for bread-making. This is a mildly sour, light-textured, well-risen loaf and is traditionally finished with a criss-cross diamond pattern on top. Bake in a steamy oven for the best result.

MAKES A 1KG (2¼LB) LOAF

500g (18oz) plus 5ml (1 tsp) organic stoneground strong white bread flour, plus extra for dusting
7.5ml (1½ tsp) salt
15ml (1 tbsp) golden caster sugar
300ml (½ pint) Easy Sourdough Starter (page 87)
175ml (6fl oz) lukewarm water

1 Put the flour, salt and sugar in a large bowl and stir together. Make a well in the middle, then add the sourdough starter and water. Mix to a soft dough.
2 Turn out the dough on a lightly floured surface and knead for 7–8 minutes until smooth and springy. Return the dough to the bowl, cover with cling film and leave to rise in a cool room (a slow rise will allow the 'friendly' bacteria to multiply, creating a better flavour) for 4–5 hours, or overnight in the fridge, until doubled in size.
3 If the dough has been refrigerated, let it come to room temperature (about an hour) before continuing. Turn the dough out on to a lightly floured surface and knead for a minute or two to deflate.

4 Shape the dough into a neat round and put on a greased baking sheet. Place in a large clean plastic bag, slightly inflate the bag and tie the end to keep it inflated. Leave it to rise at room temperature for about 2 hours, or until doubled in size.

5 Preheat the oven to 220°C (fan 200°C), gas 7. Half fill a small roasting tin with hot water and place in the bottom of the oven to create steam during cooking. Remove the loaf and tray from the plastic bag and slash the top in a diamond pattern, using a sharp knife.

6 Bake for 30–35 minutes until golden brown and hollow sounding when the base is tapped. Cool on a wire rack and serve warm or cold.

Italian Ciabatta

Ciabatta means 'slipper' in Italian and describes these flattish oval loaves. The prolonged rising and high liquid content gives the bread has a lovely light and open texture and a crisp crust. Flavoured with olive oil, the dough should be fairly wet, so don't be tempted to add more flour. After the first rise, handle very gently so that none of the air bubbles are lost. Sliced in half lengthways, ciabatta make great open sandwiches, topped with Italian ham or salami and sliced plum tomatoes.

MAKES TWO 350G (12OZ) LOAVES

350g (12oz) organic stoneground strong white bread flour, plus extra for dusting
7.5ml (1½ tsp) salt
2.5ml (½ tsp) fast-action dried yeast
300ml (½ pint) Easy Sourdough Starter (page 87)
150ml (¼ pint) lukewarm water
30ml (2 tbsp) extra virgin olive oil

1. Put the flour in a mixing bowl. Add the salt and yeast and stir to mix. Make a hollow in the middle and add the sourdough starter, water and oil. Mix together with a wooden spoon to make a dough.
2. Turn out the dough on to a lightly floured surface and knead for 7–8 minutes until soft and springy (it will be quite sticky, but don't be tempted to add more flour). Return the dough to the bowl, cover with oiled cling film and leave in a cool place for 2–3 hours, or until doubled in size.

3 Lightly dust two baking sheets with flour. Punch down the dough to deflate, then turn out on to a lightly floured surface. Cut the dough in half and shape each piece into a long oval. Place on the baking sheets, cover with oiled cling film and leave to rise for about 30 minutes.
4 Towards the end of rising time, preheat the oven to 200°C (fan 180°C), gas 6. Carefully remove the cling film and bake for 20–35 minutes, or until dark golden and hollow sounding when tapped. Transfer the loaves to a wire rack and leave to cool.

Landbrot

The name of this German country-style rye bread translates literally as 'bread of the land' and it can be found throughout Germany, although there are many regional differences, resulting in breads of different textures and colours. It keeps well and the flavour continues to mature after baking. For a lighter loaf, use equal quantities of rye and organic stoneground strong white flour.

MAKES A 1KG (2¼LB) LOAF

400g (14oz) organic stoneground wholemeal rye flour
150g (5oz) organic stoneground strong white bread flour
7.5ml (1½ tsp) fine sea salt
1.5ml (¼ tsp) ground caraway seeds
225ml (8fl oz) Easy Sourdough Starter (page 87)
about 250ml (8fl oz) warm water

1 Put the flours, salt and caraway seeds in a large bowl. Mix well and make a hollow in the middle. Add the sourdough starter and warm water and mix with your hands, gradually working in the flour. As flour and starters vary, you may need to add a little more water or white flour to make a smooth, non-sticky dough. The rye flour will make the dough feel heavy and it will be harder to work than ordinary bread dough.

2 Turn out the dough on to a lightly floured surface and knead for 7–8 minutes until smooth, or use a freestanding mixer with a dough hook for 5–6 minutes on low speed.

3 Return the dough to the bowl, cover with cling film and leave it to rise until doubled in size. This will take 4–9 hours, depending on the vigour of your starter and the room temperature; for a more flavoured bread, leave the dough at cool room temperature, as the longer it takes to rise, the more the flavour develops.

4 Punch down the dough and shape into a round. Place on a floured baking sheet and cover with oiled cling film or place the sheet in a large clean plastic bag, inflate the bag then fasten with an elastic band. For a more traditional loaf, leave the dough to rise in a canvas or wicker bread-proving basket, or a large colander lined with a clean tea towel. Leave to rise in a warm place for 3–5 hours, or until doubled in size.

5 Towards the end of the rising time, put a roasting tin of hot water on the bottom shelf of the oven to create steam and preheat the oven to 200°C (fan 180°C), gas 6. If you have used a proving basket, put a baking sheet on the centre shelf of the oven to heat.

6 Uncover the risen dough or turn the loaf out of its basket on to the hot baking sheet. Slash the top of the loaf with a sharp knife, then put in the oven and bake for 35–40 minutes or until the loaf sounds hollow when tapped underneath. Transfer to a wire rack and leave to cool.

CHAPTER 6

Cooking with Fermented Foods

Fermented foods and drinks can of course be enjoyed in their own right: a small glass of kefir, a bowl of yogurt, or a few spoonfuls of kimchi, will provide you with a good amount of beneficial bacteria. Once you have made your fermented produce, you may wish to be more adventurous and you'll soon discover that you can use them in a wide range of dishes as part of everyday eating.

In this chapter, you'll find over forty deliciously healthy recipes, from well-known classics with a new twist, to more unusual creations which will soon become favourites. As well as recipes which use your home-made ferments, you'll also find ways to enjoy fermented foods that you can buy from specialist shops, including 'natto' and 'tempeh'. Whether you choose soups, salads, mains, desserts, bakes or drinks, you'll find something here to suit, whatever the meal or occasion.

SOUPS, STARTERS AND SNACKS

Noodles in Chilled Beef Broth

All over Asia, cold noodles are eaten during the hot summer months. This classic Korean dish, 'Naengmyeon', is always served in an icy beef broth, or with a little crushed ice added just before serving. It contains a mixture of savoury and sweet ingredients, with kimchi juices balancing the flavour.

SERVES 2-3

150g (5oz) braising steak
5ml (1 tsp) sunflower or groundnut oil
few slices fresh ginger
2 spring onions, trimmed and roughly chopped
10ml (2 tsp) caster sugar
10ml (2 tsp) White Kimchi (page 34) juice
about 400ml (14fl oz) clear beef stock
200g (7oz) soba (buckwheat) noodles
2 eggs, hard-boiled
½ cucumber
1 pear, preferably an Asian pear
150g (5oz) White Kimchi (page 38)

1. Trim the meat of any fat and gristle. Heat the oil in a small frying pan until hot, then briefly fry the beef for about 45 seconds on each side until well browned. Pour in enough cold water to just cover the beef and add the ginger and spring onions.
2. Bring to a slow simmer on the lowest possible heat. Cover with a lid and cook for 30–40 minutes or until the beef is tender. Remove the meat to a board, cover and leave to cool. Remove the ginger and spring onions from the pan with a slotted spoon and discard. Skim the cooking juices, stir in the sugar and leave to cool.

3 When the liquid is cold, skim off any fat from the top, then strain into a plastic jug through a fine sieve. Stir in the kimchi juice. Make up the cooking juices to 600ml (1 pint) with the beef stock. Put the stock in the freezer to chill for an hour or so, until ice crystals start to form around the edges of the jug.

4 Meanwhile, bring a large pan of water to the boil. Add the noodles to the water a few strands at a time. Stir gently until they are all immersed in the water. Bring to a gentle boil and cook for 6–8 minutes, or following the packet instructions. Drain in a colander, then tip back into the pan and cover with cold water. When the noodles are cool, gently swish them in the water to remove any starchiness and drain again (if the water is very cloudy, rinse them again). Drain well, then loop the noodles a few at a time into neat bundles.

5 While the noodles are cooking, shell the eggs and quarter them lengthways. Carve the beef into thin slices. Cut the cucumber into fine thin strips and peel, quarter, core and thinly slice the pear. Shred the white kimchi into smaller pieces if necessary.

6 Divide the noodles between two or three bowls and top with cucumber and pear slices, then with shredded kimchi, beef and quartered eggs. Whisk the iced stock with a fork to break up any ice crystals and pour into the bowls. Serve straight away.

Notes
- Use a good-quality beef stock or broth; it should be clear, not cloudy. A can of beef consommé will work well if you don't have any stock.
- To make your own beef broth, roast 450g (1lb) beef bones in a roasting tin for 30 minutes at 190°C (fan 170°C), gas 5 until lightly browned. Tip into a large saucepan and add 1 carrot, ½ onion, 1 stick celery and 1 leek, all cleaned then roughly chopped, 1 bay leaf and 4 black peppercorns. Place on the lowest possible heat and simmer for up to 8 hours. Don't let the broth boil; it should simmer very gently with the occasional bubble or two. Leave it to cool, then strain through a fine sieve and chill in the fridge until needed.
- If you are already using the oven, cook the braising steak in a small covered ovenproof dish with the ginger and spring onions and just enough liquid to cover at 150°C (fan 130°C), gas 2 for 1½ hours; it will be very tender.

Chicken Miso Soup

This simple soup has a lovely clean flavour and is made by poaching chicken breasts, then cooking rice and carrots in the poaching stock. The miso is added to the hot soup, but not boiled, so that all the vitamins and beneficial bacteria are retained.

SERVES 2

450ml (¾ pint) light chicken stock
2 skinless chicken breasts
50g (2oz) long-grain rice
2 carrots, preferably organic, peeled and cut into 2cm (¾in) matchstick strips
3 spring onions, trimmed and finely sliced on the diagonal
15ml (1 tbsp) dark soy sauce
15ml (1 tbsp) sake or mirin (or substitute sweet sherry or white wine)
30ml (2 tbsp) brown miso paste

1 Pour the stock into a saucepan and bring to a gentle simmer. Add the chicken breasts, bring back to simmering point and cook for 7–8 minutes, or until just cooked through. Remove from the pan with a slotted spoon and transfer to a chopping board.
2 Meanwhile, rinse the rice in a sieve under cold running water. Drain well and add to the hot stock. Bring to the boil, cover the pan and simmer for 2 minutes. Add the carrots and cook for a further 6 minutes, then add the spring onions and cook for a further 1–2 minutes or until everything is tender.
3 Meanwhile, shred the chicken. Add to the pan with any juices, along with the soy sauce and sake or mirin. Gently heat until steaming hot.
4 Turn off the heat, add the miso and stir until blended. Ladle the soup into warmed bowls and serve straight away.

Notes

- Sake is a Japanese fermented rice wine. It is made by removing the bran from the rice, cooking the rice grains, then fermenting with a mould known as koji, which converts the rice starch into sugar. Yeast is added as well, to convert the sugars into alcohol at the same time.
- Miso is a fermented paste made from soya beans and sometimes rice, barley, wheat or rye. Used in Japanese and South East Asian cookery, it imparts a rich intensity and savoury flavour to any dish. It is made by soaking, cooking and mashing soya beans, then fermenting for several weeks with Aspergillus mould. The paste is then placed in a strong brine and left to ferment further. Generally, the longer it is aged, the darker the colour (from creamy-white, to yellow, orangey-red, then deep brown) and the stronger and saltier the taste. As well as beneficial bacteria, miso is rich in protein, antioxidants and vitamin B12, making it an excellent food for vegans.

Minted Pea and Broad Bean Soup with Yogurt

Starchy rice not only thickens the soup, but helps stabilise the yogurt; the mixture is blended, so you won't notice the rice when eating. Make sure you stir in the yogurt a spoonful at a time to prevent it curdling in the hot soup.

SERVES 4

25g (1oz) butter or 25ml (1½ tbsp) olive oil
1 onion, peeled and chopped
1 stick celery, sliced
30ml (2 tbsp) risotto or pudding rice
1 sprig fresh thyme (optional)
350g (12oz) shelled broad beans, fresh or frozen
1 litre (1¾ pints) chicken or vegetable stock
75g (3oz) shelled peas, fresh or frozen
100ml (4fl oz) Greek Yogurt (page 50)
60ml (4 tbsp) finely chopped fresh mint leaves
salt and freshly ground black pepper
Sourdough Loaf (page 84) and Cultured Butter (page 57), to serve

1. Melt the butter or heat the oil in a large saucepan. Add the onion and gently fry for 5 minutes, stirring frequently. Add the celery and cook for a few more minutes, or until the onion is soft.
2. Add the rice and stir well, then add the thyme, if using, and broad beans. Pour over the stock, bring to the boil and simmer for 5 minutes. Add the peas and cook for a further 5 minutes, or until the rice is tender.
3. Remove the thyme and discard. Puree the soup in a blender or food processor (in batches if necessary) or use a hand blender to puree in the pan. Reheat the soup until piping hot, then turn off the heat. Add the yogurt a tablespoon at a time, stirring well between each addition, then stir in most of the mint.
4. Taste and season with salt and pepper, then ladle into warmed bowls. Sprinkle with the remaining chopped mint and serve straight away with warm sourdough bread and cultured butter.

Borscht

This beetroot soup is a classic of Russia and Poland (where it is known as 'barszcz'). There are many versions ranging from a basic beetroot broth to more elaborate soups with meat, beans and root vegetables.

SERVES 4

25g (1oz) butter or 25ml (1½ tbsp) sunflower oil
1 onion, peeled and finely chopped
1 medium carrot, peeled and diced
1 stick celery, chopped
350g (12oz) beetroot, peeled and diced
1.5 litres (2½ pints) beef stock
1 bay leaf
2 small potatoes, peeled and diced
½ small white cabbage, finely shredded
1 garlic clove, peeled and crushed
5ml (1 tsp) dark muscovado sugar (optional)
75ml (5 tbsp) Beetroot Kvass (page 79)
salt and freshly ground black pepper
Soured Cream (page 56) and snipped fresh chives or chopped fresh dill, to serve

1. Melt the butter or heat the oil in a large heavy-based saucepan and gently fry the onion for 5 minutes until beginning to soften. Add the carrot, celery and beetroot and cook for a further 2–3 minutes, stirring frequently.
2. Pour in the stock, add the bay leaf and bring to the boil. Lower the heat, part-cover the pan with a lid and gently simmer for 10 minutes.
3. Add the potatoes and cook for a further 10 minutes, then add the cabbage, garlic and sugar, if using. Cook for a further 12–15 minutes, until all the vegetables are very tender.
4. Remove the bay leaf, stir in the kvass, season with salt and pepper and ladle the soup into warmed bowls. Serve topped with soured cream and a sprinkling of chives or dill.

Thai-style Vegetable Omelette

Here, eggs are whisked with a little cornflour to make the omelettes firmer and more flexible. They have a colourful filling of stir-fried vegetables and kimchi.

SERVES 4

20ml (4 tsp) cornflour
45ml (3 tbsp) cold filtered water
8 eggs
1.5ml (¼ tsp) red chilli flakes (optional)
30ml (2 tbsp) sunflower oil
100g (4oz) fine rice noodles
100g (4oz) mushrooms, sliced
1 small yellow pepper, deseeded and cut into thin strips
225g (8oz) Kimchi (page 34), drained
15ml (1 tbsp) soy sauce

1. Blend the cornflour and water in a bowl. Add the eggs and chilli flakes, if using, and whisk together until mixed.
2. Heat 5ml (1 tsp) of the oil in a 20cm (8in) non-stick frying pan. Pour in a quarter of the egg mixture, tipping the pan and swirling the mixture to spread out into a thin even layer. Cook for about 2 minutes until golden brown underneath and lightly set.
3. Slide the omelette out of the pan on to a warmed plate. Make three more omelettes in the same way, stacking them up with baking parchment or greaseproof paper between them. Keep warm.
4. Soak the rice noodles in a heatproof bowl with boiling water for 4 minutes or according to the packet instructions, then drain well.
5. Meanwhile, heat the remaining oil in a wok or large frying pan. Add the mushrooms and yellow pepper and stir-fry for 3–4 minutes or until tender. Add the noodles, most of the kimchi and the soy sauce and stir-fry for a further 1–2 minutes or until heated through.
6. Turn off the heat and stir in the remaining kimchi (adding this later retains the beneficial bacteria). Divide the mixture between the four omelettes and fold them in half. Serve straight away.

Griddled Asparagus with Yogurt Hollandaise

Despite its simplicity, asparagus with a hollandaise sauce makes a fabulous starter or light lunch. It can also be served as a vegetable accompaniment to fish such as salmon. Here, it is made with yogurt instead of butter for a healthier dish.

SERVES 2 AS A STARTER OR LIGHT LUNCH, 4 AS A VEGETABLE ACCOMPANIMENT

250g (9oz) asparagus spears
15ml (1 tbsp) extra virgin olive oil
15g (½oz) toasted flaked almonds

For the yogurt hollandaise
150ml (¼ pint) plain yogurt (page 49)
5ml (1 tsp) lemon juice
2 egg yolks
5ml (1 tsp) Dijon mustard
salt and freshly ground black pepper

1. To make the hollandaise, beat together the yogurt, lemon juice, egg yolks, mustard and a little salt and pepper in a heatproof bowl.
2. Place the bowl over a pan of barely simmering water and cook, stirring, for 15 minutes or until thick. (The sauce will become thinner partway through cooking, then will thicken.) Turn off the heat but leave the bowl over the hot water, stirring now and then, while cooking the asparagus.
3. Cook the asparagus spears in boiling salted water for 2–3 minutes; they should be barely tender but retain a little 'bite'. Drain well and toss in the olive oil.
4. Meanwhile, heat a ridged griddle pan until very hot. Place the spears on the griddle and cook for 2–3 minutes, turning to get a striped charred effect.
5. Divide the asparagus between warmed plates (not too hot, or the hollandaise will curdle). Spoon the hollandaise over the asparagus and sprinkle with toasted flaked almonds. Serve straight away.

EASY MEZZE

Mezze is a selection of small dishes that can be served to accompany drinks, as a starter or as a meal in its own right. The following are all made with cultured and fermented food. You don't need to make them all; pick two or three, depending on the occasion and how many you are serving, and add other items as well, such as bowls of olives, mini koftas, vegetable crudités and breadsticks, warmed flatbreads or pittas, cut into fingers for dipping.

Each of the recipe serves 4 as a starter or 6–8 as part of a mezze selection.

Tzatziki

This yogurt dip can be served with sticks of raw carrots or peppers, with pitta bread, or as an accompaniment to grilled meat or kofte (meatballs).

> 1 cucumber
> 300ml (½ pint) Greek Yogurt (page 50)
> 5ml (1 tsp) olive oil
> 30ml (2 tbsp) chopped fresh mint
> 1 garlic clove, peeled and crushed
> salt and freshly ground black pepper

1. Halve, deseed and dice the cucumber. Place in a sieve, sprinkling over a little salt as you go, then leave to drain over a bowl for 20 minutes (the salt will extract some of the juices).
2. Discard the cucumber juice, then wipe the bowl clean with kitchen paper. Tip the drained cucumber into the bowl, add the yogurt, oil, mint, garlic and some pepper. Mix well and chill until ready to serve.

Smoked Aubergine and Yogurt Dip

This is a less oily version of the Greek 'melitzanosalata'; it uses yogurt instead of some of the olive oil. Serve with warmed pittas or flatbreads.

> 2 medium aubergines, about 450g (1lb) in total
> 2 garlic cloves
> 25g (1oz) ground almonds
> 15ml (1 tbsp) extra virgin olive oil
> 15ml (1 tbsp) lemon juice
> 5ml (1 tsp) ground cumin
> salt and freshly ground black pepper
> 150ml (¼ pint) plain yogurt (page 49)

1 Preheat the oven to 180°C (fan 160°C), gas 4. Prick the aubergines several times with a fork and place on a lightly greased baking tray. Bake for 45 minutes, turning two or three times, then add the garlic to the tray and bake for a further 15 minutes or until the aubergines are very soft and charred (this gives them the smoky flavour). Remove from the oven and leave until cool enough to handle, then quarter lengthways and peel off the skin.

2 Chop the aubergine flesh and leave to drain in a colander for 15 minutes, then, using your hands, squeeze out as much liquid as possible. Put in a food processor and add the garlic, squeezed out of its papery skin, almonds, olive oil, lemon juice and cumin. Season with salt and pepper and blend until smooth. Add the yogurt and briefly blend again. Spoon into a bowl and chill until ready to serve.

Creamy Hummus

Delicious with an array of raw vegetables for dipping – or try hummus in a wrap with falafels.

400g (14fl oz) can chickpeas, drained and rinsed
1 garlic clove, peeled and crushed
30ml (2 tbsp) lemon juice
30ml (2 tbsp) tahini (sesame seed paste)
2.5ml (½ tsp) ground cumin, plus extra for sprinkling
75ml (5 tbsp) Milk Kefir (page 62)
salt and freshly ground black pepper

1. Put the chickpeas, garlic, lemon juice, tahini, cumin and kefir in a food processor. Season with salt and pepper and blend for 2 minutes, or until very smooth, stopping and scraping down the sides of the processor once or twice.
2. Spoon the hummus into a bowl, cover and chill in the fridge. Sprinkle with a pinch of cumin just before serving.

Yogurt-spiced Chicken Skewers

The yogurt tenderises the chicken while the spices add flavour. For a light lunch or supper dish, serve with salad in warmed pittas or flatbreads.

200ml (7fl oz) plain yogurt (page 49)
5ml (1 tsp) ground cumin
5ml (1 tsp) ground coriander
2.5ml (½ tsp) ground turmeric
2.5ml (½ tsp) ground ginger
1.5ml (¼ tsp) chilli powder
2.5ml (½ tsp) salt
2 skinless boneless chicken breasts
Fermented Mango Preserve (page 45), to serve

1. Stir the yogurt, cumin, coriander, turmeric, ginger, chilli powder and salt together in a bowl. Slice each chicken breast in half horizontally, then cut lengthways into 2cm (¾in) strips. Add to the spicy yogurt mixture, stir well, cover the bowl with cling film and leave to marinate in the fridge for at least 1 hour and up to 4 hours.
2. Meanwhile, soak eight wooden skewers (kebab sticks) in cold water (this will stop them burning during cooking). Preheat the grill to high. Thread the chicken, concertina-style, on to the skewers and cook under the hot grill for 3 minutes on each side until browned and cooked through. Serve with mango preserve or chutney.

Kefir Ranch-style Dip

Serve with sticks of carrot, celery, pepper or courgette, with tortilla chips or strips of pitta bread, or on baked potatoes.

200ml (7fl oz) Milk Kefir (page 62)
75g (3oz) mayonnaise
10ml (2 tsp) snipped fresh dill
10ml (2 tsp) chopped fresh parsley
1 garlic clove, peeled and crushed
salt and freshly ground black pepper

1. Line a large sieve or colander with a double layer of muslin (cheesecloth) and place over a bowl. Pour the kefir into the muslin and leave to drain for at least 12 hours and up to 24 hours until very thick, like a soft cream cheese.
2. Tip the drained kefir into a bowl (you can drink the whey or use it in another recipe) and add the mayonnaise, dill, parsley and garlic. Season with salt and pepper and mix well. Cover and chill for at least an hour before serving.

Marinated Herring and Beetroot Salad

This Scandinavian-style salad is an excellent way to use up beetroot after making kvass. You can buy jars of marinated herring in dill or white wine marinades. Herring is high in omega-3 and can help lower blood pressure and protect against heart disease.

SERVES 4

250g (9oz) jar of marinated herring, diced
175g (6oz) diced beetroot, left over after making and straining Beetroot Kvass (page 79)
1 red-skinned eating apple, quartered, cored and diced
15ml (1 tbsp) mayonnaise
30ml (2 tbsp) Greek Yogurt (page 50), Soured Cream (page 56) or Crème Fraiche (page 56)
10ml (2 tsp) creamed horseradish sauce
freshly ground black pepper
bag of mixed baby salad leaves, such as beetroot leaves, small red chard leaves and rocket
slices of Sourdough loaf (page 84) or rye bread, to serve

1 Put the herring, beetroot and apple in a bowl. Blend together the mayonnaise, yogurt, soured cream or crème fraiche and horseradish sauce, seasoning with a little black pepper. Add to the bowl and mix together well.
2 Place the baby salad leaves in a wide shallow bowl and pile the herring and beetroot mixture on top. Serve straight away with slices of sourdough or rye bread.

Note
If you don't have beetroot left over from making kvass, use 175g (6oz) Pickled Beetroot and Turnips (page 40) instead.

Smoked Salmon and Pasta Salad with Avocado Kefir Dressing

This colourful substantial salad contains a range of contrasting tastes and textures brought together with a creamy avocado and kefir dressing. Smoked salmon, like other oily fish, is a rich source of omega-3, which can help to protect against high blood pressure and heart disease.

SERVES 4

250g (9oz) white or wholemeal farfalle (pasta bows)
100g (4oz) frozen soya beans, defrosted
100ml (4fl oz) Milk Kefir (page 62)
1 small ripe avocado, stoned and roughly chopped
100g (4oz) watercress
2 spring onions, roughly chopped
salt and freshly ground black pepper
30ml (2 tbsp) capers, drained
¼ cucumber, diced
100g (4oz) smoked salmon, cut into thin strips

1. Cook the pasta in boiling lightly salted water for 10–12 minutes, or according to the packet instructions, until al dente, adding the soya beans 2 minutes before the end of cooking time. Drain in a colander, lightly rinse with cold water, then drain again. Tip into a bowl.
2. While the pasta is cooking, put the kefir and avocado in a food processor or blender and blend until smooth.
3. Add 50g (2oz) of the watercress and the spring onions and season with a little salt and pepper. Process again until the watercress and spring onions are very finely chopped and the sauce has a speckled appearance. Stir in the capers.
4. Add the dressing to the pasta and soya beans and mix well. Divide among four plates, adding the remaining watercress and the cucumber as you pile the salad on to the plates. Arrange the smoked salmon on top and serve.

Summer Chicken Caesar Salad

Full of flavour and contrasting textures, this salad includes crunchy green beans and baby courgettes. If you prefer, use a yogurt dressing or kefir dressing instead of the Caesar dressing (see Variations).

SERVES 4

50g (2oz) can anchovy fillets
1 garlic clove, peeled and crushed
6 thin slices of Sourdough Loaf (page 84)
100g (4oz) fine green beans, trimmed
2 baby courgettes, cut into 1cm (½in) slices
2 small cos lettuces, about 400g (14oz) in total, torn into bite-sized pieces
2 cooked skinned boneless chicken breasts, cut into 2cm (¾in) chunks
25g (1oz) Parmesan cheese shavings

For the Caesar dressing
5ml (1 tsp) Dijon mustard
45ml (3 tbsp) extra virgin olive oil
10ml (2 tsp) white wine vinegar
30ml (2 tbsp) plain yogurt (page 49)
dash Worcestershire sauce
freshly ground black pepper

1 Preheat the oven to 200°C (fan 180°C), gas 6. Put the anchovies in a bowl with the oil from the can. Add the garlic and mash to a smooth paste with a fork. Spread thinly over one side of each piece of sourdough. Put on a baking sheet and bake for about 10 minutes or until crisp and golden. Leave to cool.

2 Cook the beans and courgettes in a saucepan of lightly salted boiling water for 3–4 minutes or until just tender. Drain and tip into a bowl of cold water, leave to cool for a minute then drain again. Wipe the bowl dry. Tip the cooked vegetables into the bowl and add the lettuce and chicken.
3 While the bread and vegetables are cooking, make the dressing. Whisk together the mustard, oil, vinegar, yogurt, Worcestershire sauce and black pepper. Pour half the dressing over the chicken mixture and gently mix together.
4 Break the toasted bread into smaller pieces and add to the salad. Mix again, then drizzle over the rest of the dressing and scatter with shaved Parmesan. Serve straight away.

Variations

- For a yogurt dressing, mix 100ml (4fl oz) Greek Yogurt (page 50) with 15ml (1 tbsp) lemon juice, 10ml (2 tsp) white wine vinegar, salt and pepper.
- You can leave the yogurt dressing plain or add flavourings, e.g. add 5ml (1 tsp) tomato puree for seafood salad, add 10ml (2 tsp) creamed horseradish for beef or smoked fish such as mackerel salad, add 15ml (1 tbsp) chopped fresh herbs such as coriander or basil for pasta salad, or tarragon or chives for chicken salad.
- For a kefir ranch-style dressing, mix 60ml (4 tbsp) mayonnaise, 60ml (4 tbsp) Milk Kefir (page 62), 10ml (2 tsp) olive oil, 1 small crushed clove garlic, 1.5ml (¼ tsp) dried herbs (chives, parsley and dill), and a pinch of salt and pepper.

Salmon and Kimchi Sushi Rolls

Although Korean and Japanese food are very different, kimchi is an excellent flavouring for sushi, and the tart fermenting juices can be used to replace the classic flavouring of rice wine vinegar.

MAKES 32 SUSHI ROLLS

300g (11oz) sushi rice
450ml (¾ pint) boiling water
5ml (1 tsp) caster sugar
45ml (3 tbsp) Kimchi (page 34) juice
100g (4oz) smoked salmon
4 sheets of sushi nori, about 10g (scant ½oz) in total
10ml (2 tsp) wasabi paste (optional)
100g (4oz) drained Kimchi (page 34), any larger pieces finely shredded
soy sauce, for dipping

1 Put the rice and boiling water in a medium-sized saucepan. Bring to the boil, then lower the heat, cover the pan and simmer for 20 minutes, or until almost all the water has been absorbed. Turn off the heat and leave to stand for 10 minutes; the rice will absorb any remaining liquid.

2 Mix together the sugar and kimchi juice until most of the sugar has dissolved. Drizzle over the warm rice and stir well. Cover the pan with a tea towel and leave to cool.

3 Divide the sushi rice into four equal portions. Cut the salmon into strips about 1cm (½in wide). Put a sheet of nori, shiny side down, on a bamboo sushi mat or on a sheet of baking parchment on a chopping board. Spread a portion of rice over the nori, leaving a small space at the top and bottom. Put a quarter of the salmon on top, spread with a little of the wasabi, if using, then top with a quarter of the kimchi.

4 Using the bamboo mat or parchment, tightly roll up the nori. Make three more rolls in the same way. Use a very sharp wet knife to cut each roll into eight equal-sized slices and place them filling-side up on a serving plate. Wipe the knife in between cuts with a damp paper towel to keep the knife clean. Chill until ready to serve, with soy sauce for dipping.

Fresh Tomato and Kefir Cheese Bruschetta

These tasty sourdough toasts are topped with tangy kefir cheese flavoured with olives and mint and topped with a fresh tomato salsa. They make a delicious canapé, snack or light lunch.

SERVES 4

15ml (1 tbsp) balsamic vinegar
30ml (2 tbsp) olive oil
freshly ground black pepper
8 ripe tomatoes, peeled (see Note), coarsely chopped and drained
½ small red onion, peeled and finely chopped
2 garlic cloves, peeled and crushed
8 slices of Sourdough Loaf (page 84), cut 1cm (½cm) thick, about 350g (12oz) in total
200g (7oz) Kefir Soft Cheese (page 66)
50g (2oz) stoned green olives, chopped
45ml (3 tbsp) chopped fresh mint

1. Whisk together the balsamic vinegar, olive oil and a little black pepper in a bowl. Add the tomatoes, onion and garlic and mix well. Cover with cling film and refrigerate for at least an hour to allow the flavours to mellow and blend.
2. Heat a large, ridged cast-iron grill pan over a moderately high heat. Add four slices of the bread and toast for about 2 minutes or until crisp and lightly marked with stripes. Turn the bread over and toast the other side. Repeat with the remaining four slices of bread.
3. Put the kefir cheese in a bowl with the chopped olives and mint. Mix well. Pile on top of the toasts, dividing evenly, then make a slight hollow in the middle of the cheese. Spoon the tomato mixture on top and serve straight away.

Note
To peel tomatoes, put them in a heatproof bowl and cover with boiling water. Leave for 45 seconds to a minute or until the skins start to peel, then drain and rinse under cold water. The skins should now peel away easily.

Variation
If you prefer, use 150g (5oz) antipasto peppers from a jar instead of the tomato mixture, draining well and chopping into slightly smaller pieces to make sure the bruschetta is easy to eat.

Couscous and Grilled Pepper Salad with Labneh

Couscous is one of the simplest grains to prepare and can be served hot or cold. Here, it is combined with colourful grilled peppers and topped with little labneh cheeses. A creamy tahini dressing adds the finishing touch.

SERVES 4

200g (7oz) couscous
300ml (½ pint) boiling vegetable stock or water
3 peppers, preferably 1 yellow, 1 orange and 1 red (do not use green; they can be bitter when grilled)
200g (7oz) canned chickpeas, drained and rinsed
1 batch Labneh (page 51)

For the tahini dressing
15ml (1 tbsp) tahini (stir well before spooning from the jar)
juice of 1 large lemon
1 garlic clove, peeled and crushed
10ml (2 tsp) extra virgin olive oil
salt and freshly ground black pepper

1. Put the couscous in a heatproof bowl and pour over the stock or water. Stir, then cover with a pan lid or a clean tea towel and leave to stand for at least 15 minutes.
2. Meanwhile, preheat the grill to high and line the tray with foil. Quarter the peppers and remove the seeds and membranes. Place on the grill tray, skin-side up, and grill for about 5–10 minutes until charred and blistered. Move them around the tray if necessary to char them evenly. Remove from the grill and wrap the peppers in the foil to seal in the steam. Leave for about 10 minutes, then peel off the skin and thickly slice the peppers.

3 Alternatively, you can cook the peppers in the oven. Preheat the oven to 200°C (fan 180°C), gas 6. Lightly brush the whole peppers with oil and arrange in a shallow roasting tin. Roast for 30 minutes, turning them two or three times. Place the hot peppers in a polythene bag and leave until cool enough to handle. Cut them in half, discard the cores and seeds, then cut into thick slices.
4 For the dressing, whisk together the tahini, lemon juice, garlic and olive oil.
5 Fork through the couscous to separate, then add the peppers and chickpeas. Drizzle over half of the dressing and gently stir together. Taste and season with salt and pepper. Spoon into a serving dish or individual bowls. Top with the labneh cheese, then drizzle over the remaining dressing.

Sesame Chicken Salad

Marinating in buttermilk makes poultry and meat juicy and tender; the combination of enzymes and acids works together to start to break down the protein. Here, strips of chicken are tenderised before being coated in a mixture of breadcrumbs and sesame seeds. They are then oven-baked to give a crisp golden finish without the fat and calories of frying.

SERVES 4

450g (1lb) skinless boneless chicken breasts
150ml (¼ pint) Buttermilk (page 57)
1.5ml (½ tsp) salt
75g (3oz) fresh white breadcrumbs; use sourdough loaf (page 84) breadcrumbs if you prefer
30ml (2 tbsp) sesame seeds
5ml (1 tsp) smoked paprika
2.5ml (½ tsp) hot chilli powder (optional)
freshly ground black pepper
2 eggs
225g (8oz) Mixed Vegetable Slaw (page 26) with dressing
60g (2½oz) bag baby salad leaves

1. Preheat the oven to 200°C (fan 180°C), gas 6. Slice each chicken breast in half horizontally, then cut lengthways into 2cm (¾in) strips. Mix together the buttermilk and salt in a bowl, add the chicken and stir to coat all the pieces. Cover the bowl with cling film and leave to marinate in the fridge for at least 1 hour and up to 3 hours.
2. Drain the chicken well, discarding the buttermilk. Put the breadcrumbs, sesame seeds, paprika, chilli powder, if using, and black pepper into a mixing bowl and stir well. Whisk the eggs together on a plate.

3 Dip each chicken strip first into the beaten egg, then into the breadcrumb mixture. Place on a large (or you can use two smaller ones) lightly greased non-stick baking tray, spacing slightly apart. If you have an oil spray, spray the chicken with a very light coating of oil.
4 Bake the chicken strips for 15–18 minutes, turning the pieces halfway through cooking time, until golden brown and just cooked through (don't overcook or the chicken will be dry).
5 While the chicken is cooking, mix together the dressed vegetable slaw and baby salad leaves. Divide between four plates. Pile the chicken on top and serve straight away.

Variation

The chicken strips can also be served with a blue cheese dip. Blend 50g (2oz) blue cheese, e.g. Stilton or Roquefort, with 50g (2oz) Kefir Soft Cheese (page 66), 150ml (¼ pint) Buttermilk (page 57), salt and pepper. If liked, stir in some chopped fresh herbs such as chives, tarragon or parsley.

Quinoa Falafels in Wholemeal Pittas with Mixed Vegetable Slaw

Quinoa has a fantastic nutritional profile when compared to other grains and it contains all nine essential amino acids, making it a good choice for vegans and vegetarians. It is also low in fat and cholesterol-free. Here, it is combined with chickpeas – also high in protein – to make tasty little falafels to serve in pittas. Baking destroys the beneficial bacteria in the yogurt used to make the pittas, but it does give them a lovely soft texture.

SERVES 4

For the olive and coriander wholemeal pittas
150g (5oz) wholemeal strong bread flour, preferably organic
100g (4oz) strong white bread flour, preferably organic
7g (¼oz) sachet easy-blend dried yeast
5ml (1 tsp) fine sea salt
100ml (4fl oz) plain yogurt (page 49)
45ml (3 tbsp) warm water
15ml (1 tbsp) extra virgin olive oil
15ml (1 tbsp) chopped fresh coriander
25g (1oz) pitted black olives, chopped

For the falafels
45ml (3 tbsp) sunflower oil
1 small onion, peeled and finely chopped
2 garlic cloves, peeled and crushed
65g (2½oz) pearl quinoa
5ml (1 tsp) ground cumin
5ml (1 tsp) ground coriander
200ml (7fl oz) vegetable stock or water
200g (7oz) canned chickpeas, drained and rinsed
10ml (2 tsp) tahini
salt and freshly ground black pepper
30ml (2 tbsp) chopped fresh coriander
quinoa flour, wholemeal flour or plain flour, for coating
100g (4oz) Mixed Vegetable Slaw (page 26)
60ml (4 tbsp) yogurt dressing (page 113)

1 To make the pittas, put the flours in a mixing bowl, add the yeast and salt and mix well. Make a hollow in the middle. Stir the yogurt, warm water and oil together in a jug, pour into the hollow, then mix to a soft dough.
2 Turn out the dough on to a lightly floured surface and cover with an upturned bowl. Leave to rest for 5 minutes, then knead the dough for 5 minutes until smooth. Flatten the dough into a round and sprinkle with the coriander and olives. Fold the dough over to enclose the fresh ingredients, then knead the dough for 2–3 minutes, until they are evenly distributed. Return the dough to the bowl, cover with cling film and leave to rise in a warm place for about an hour, until doubled in size.
3 Turn out the dough, punch down with your knuckles, then divide into four pieces. Shape each into a ball, cover with cling film and leave to rest for 10 minutes. Roll out each ball to an oval shape about 18cm (7in) long and 5mm (¼in) thick. Arrange the breads on a greased baking sheet, cover with oiled cling film and leave to rise for 30 minutes.
4 While the pittas are rising, preheat the oven to 230°C (fan 210°C), gas 8. Spray or sprinkle the pittas with water and bake for 4–5 minutes. Transfer to a wire rack and cover with a tea towel to keep them soft.
5 While the pittas are proving and baking, make the falafels. Heat 15ml (1 tbsp) of the oil in a saucepan and gently cook the onion for 5 minutes until almost soft. Stir in the garlic, quinoa, cumin and ground coriander and cook over a low heat for 1 minute. Pour in the vegetable stock or water, stir, then cover with a lid and cook on a low heat for 20 minutes or until all of the stock or water has been absorbed. Turn off the heat, remove the lid and leave until barely warm.

6 Tip the quinoa mixture into a food processor, add the chickpeas and tahini and season with salt and pepper. Pulse the food processor until the mixture is blended but not completely smooth, adding the chopped fresh coriander towards the end of blending.
7 Using your hands, shape the mixture into 16 balls, using a little flour if needed to stop your hands getting sticky. Heat the remaining 30ml (2 tbsp) oil in a frying pan and fry the falafels for 5–7 minutes, turning occasionally to ensure even browning (if your frying pan isn't large enough, you may need to do this in two batches). Drain the falafels on kitchen paper.
8 Split open the warm pittas and fill with the falafels and mixed vegetable slaw, tossed in yogurt dressing. Serve warm.

Creamy Seafood Wraps with Kimchi

Kimchi makes a great alternative to a side salad and the flavour works really well with seafood, making a slightly vinegary accompaniment and a contrast in texture. Use a thick kefir cheese for the filling as the juices will dilute it a little as they cook. Make sure the wraps are just heated through, but not overcooked, to retain some of the beneficial bacteria in the cheese.

SERVES 4

4 ripe tomatoes, peeled (see page 117) and diced
4 spring onions, trimmed and finely sliced
175g (6oz) Kefir Soft Cheese (page 66)
freshly ground black pepper
250g (9oz) ready-to-eat seafood mix including prawns, mussels and squid, defrosted and well drained, if frozen
4 large soft flour tortillas
50g (2oz) mature Cheddar, grated
White Kimchi (page 38) or Classic Kimchi (page 34), to serve

1. Preheat the oven to 200°C (fan 180°C), gas 6. Put the tomatoes and spring onions in a bowl. Add the kefir cheese and a little black pepper and mix together. Add the seafood, then carefully mix, taking care not to break up the seafood too much.
2. Lay the tortillas on a board, then spoon and spread over the filling as evenly as possible, to within 2.5cm (1in) of the edges; don't worry if there are a few gaps.
3. Roll up the tortillas and place in a lightly oiled ovenproof dish. Sprinkle the grated Cheddar over the top, then cover with foil. Bake for 15–20 minutes, or until heated through, removing the foil for the last few minutes to allow the cheese to brown.
4. Remove the wraps from the dish, cut each in half and serve straight away, accompanied by white or classic kimchi.

MAIN MEALS

Mango-stuffed Chicken Breasts

This stylish dish is great for dinner-party dining and can be prepared in advance. It doesn't take a lot of time to make or cook. Serve extra mango preserve on the side, so that you benefit from those 'good for you' bacteria.

SERVES 4

4 skinless boneless chicken breasts, about 150g (5oz) each
100g (4oz) mozzarella cheese, thinly sliced
100g (4oz) Fermented Mango Preserve (page 45), plus extra to serve
45ml (3 tbsp) roughly chopped fresh coriander
salt and freshly ground black pepper
4 slices Parma ham, about 50g (2oz) in total
15ml (1 tbsp) extra virgin olive oil
noodles or rice and green vegetables, to serve

1. Make a slit along the length of each chicken breast, cutting almost but not all the way through to make a pocket.
2. Divide the mozzarella between the chicken breasts, sliding it into the pockets. Chop the mango preserve finely and mix with the coriander. Divide between the pockets.
3. Season the chicken breasts with salt and pepper, then wrap each in a slice of Parma ham, making sure that the ham covers the slit to hold in the filling during cooking. Tie the ham securely in place with several pieces of string or use wooden cocktail sticks. The chicken can now be kept in a covered dish in the fridge for up to 8 hours or until ready to cook.

4 Preheat the oven to 220°C (fan 200°C), gas 7. Heat the oil in a non-stick frying pan, add the chicken breasts and fry over a high heat for 2 minutes on each side until browned.
5 Transfer the chicken to an ovenproof dish, cover with foil to keep the chicken moist and bake for 10–12 minutes; the juices should run clear when the chicken is pierced with a skewer or thin knife.
6 Remove from the oven and let the chicken 'rest' for a few minutes, then remove the string or cocktail sticks and cut each breast into thick slices. Arrange on warmed plates and serve with noodles or rice and steamed green vegetables. Add a spoonful of fermented mango preserve to each plate.

Hunter's Stew

Considered by many as Poland's national dish, this is also known as 'bigos' and usually contains several different kinds of meat, originally whatever the hunter returned home with. Although there is no strict recipe, it always contains a mixture of fresh cabbage and sauerkraut. Here, some sauerkraut is reserved and added at the end of cooking to retain the beneficial bacteria.

SERVES 4

10g (scant ½oz) dried porcini mushrooms
30ml (2 tbsp) sunflower oil
1 onion, peeled and sliced
5ml (1 tsp) juniper berries, crushed
2.5ml (½ tsp) caraway seeds
10ml (2 tsp) soft brown sugar (optional)
350g (12oz) lean braising steak, pork or venison (or a mixture), cut into 2cm (¾in) chunks
450g (1lb) Sauerkraut (page 23)
200g (7oz) peeled and chopped fresh tomatoes or a 400g (14oz) can chopped tomatoes
half a small white cabbage, shredded
400ml (14fl oz) beef or vegetable stock (depending on the meat you use)
175g (6oz) smoked Polish sausage, such as kabanos or kielbasa, chopped
freshly ground black pepper

1. Put the mushrooms in a small bowl and pour over boiling water to completely cover. Leave for 5 minutes, then remove the mushrooms with a slotted spoon (rather than just draining, so that any grit is left behind). Rinse out the bowl, return the mushrooms and cover again with boiling water. Leave to soak.
2. Heat the oil in a large flameproof casserole. Add the onion and cook over a medium heat for about 5 minutes or until the onion is soft. Sprinkle over the juniper berries and caraway seeds and brown sugar, if using. Add the meat, then turn up the heat to high for a couple of minutes and cook, stirring frequently until the meat browns.
3. Drain the sauerkraut well (returning the juices to the jar, so that you can use them in another dish or ferment). Add three quarters to the casserole with the tomatoes, white cabbage and stock. Bring to the boil, lower the heat and simmer for 30 minutes.
4. Add the Polish sausage, mushrooms and the soaking water to the casserole. Season with black pepper, cover and simmer for a further 1½ hours or until the meat is very tender. You can serve straight away, but the flavour is better if left to cool, then refrigerated overnight and served reheated the following day. Stir in the remaining sauerkraut just before serving; once added do not re-boil.

Paprika Pork

This meal-in-a-bowl is a cross between a soup and a casserole and contains all the essential flavours of a goulash. It is topped with tiny dumplings, but not the heavy suet-based kind – these are simpler and made with breadcrumbs and fresh parsley.

SERVES 4

30ml (2 tbsp) sunflower oil
450g (1lb) lean stewing pork, trimmed and cut into 2cm (¾in) cubes
1 large onion, peeled and thinly sliced
2 garlic cloves, peeled and crushed
15ml (1 tbsp) smoked paprika
600ml (1 pint) beef stock
15ml (1 tbsp) Worcestershire sauce
2 large carrots, peeled and chopped
400g (14oz) can chopped tomatoes
1.5ml (¼ tsp) caraway seeds
salt and freshly ground black pepper
150g (5oz) Spiced Red Cabbage and Apple Sauerkraut (page 25), drained
30ml (2 tbsp) sauerkraut juice (from the jar)

For the dumplings
15ml (1 tbsp) sunflower oil
1 small onion, peeled and finely chopped
1 egg
45ml (3 tbsp) milk
45ml (3 tbsp) chopped fresh parsley
150g (5oz) Sourdough Loaf (page 84) breadcrumbs
Soured Cream (page 56) and extra paprika, to serve

1 Heat 15ml (1 tbsp) of the oil in a large frying pan and fry the cubes of pork for 2–3 minutes, stirring over a high heat until browned. Transfer to a large saucepan.

2. Add the remaining 15ml (1 tbsp) oil to the frying pan, add the onion and cook over a low heat for 5 minutes, stirring frequently. Add the garlic and fry for a further 2–3 minutes or until the onion is fairly soft. Sprinkle over the paprika and stir for a few seconds, then stir in a little stock. Tip the mixture into the saucepan.
3. Add the rest of the stock, Worcestershire sauce, carrots, chopped tomatoes and caraway seeds. Season with salt and pepper (don't add too much salt as the sauerkraut is already salted). Stir well and bring to the boil, then lower the heat, cover and simmer gently for 50 minutes to 1 hour, or until the pork is just tender.
4. Stir in the sauerkraut (but not the juice at this stage) and bring back to simmering point while making the dumplings.
5. To make the dumplings, wipe out the frying pan with kitchen paper, then gently cook the onion in the oil for 10 minutes, until tender. Turn off the heat and leave to cool for a few minutes. Beat the egg and milk together in a bowl, then add the onion, parsley and breadcrumbs. Season with salt and pepper and mix well.
6. Shape the mixture into 12 small balls, then add to the saucepan. Cover with a lid and simmer for a further 15 minutes or until the dumplings are cooked through. Turn off the heat. When the casserole stops bubbling, lift out the dumplings with a slotted spoon and place on a warmed plate.
7. Stir the sauerkraut juice into the pork (don't re-boil or you will destroy the beneficial bacteria), then ladle into warmed deep bowls. Place the dumplings on one side and top the pork with a spoonful of soured cream and a sprinkling of paprika. Serve straight away.

Note

Worcestershire sauce is a fermented sauce originally created in the nineteenth century to disguise less-than-fresh meat! It is a thin, dark brown sauce made by fermenting a wide range of ingredients including anchovies, shallots, garlic, soy sauce, tamarind, salt and vinegar.

Mediterranean Lamb Kebabs

Yogurt is the key to the marinade for these juicy kebabs, as it helps to start breaking down the protein in the meat, making it tender and succulent. Combined with fresh vegetables, some simple steamed rice or warmed pitta bread is all that is needed to make this a tasty main meal.

SERVES 4

150ml (¼ pint) plain yogurt (page 49), plus extra for serving
15ml (1 tbsp) olive oil
15ml (1 tbsp) bottled mint sauce
400g (14oz) lean lamb neck fillets, trimmed and cut into 2.5cm (1in) cubes
8 shallots, peeled
2 courgettes, about 400g (14oz) in total
1 aubergine, about 225g (8oz)
salt and freshly ground black pepper
steamed or boiled rice, to serve

1. Mix together the yogurt, oil and mint sauce in a bowl. Add the cubes of lamb and coat them in the mixture, then cover the bowl with cling film and leave to marinate in a cool place for 30 minutes or for up to 12 hours in the fridge.
2. Cut each shallot in half lengthways through the root. Cut each courgette into eight slices and cut the aubergine in half lengthways, then each half into eight pieces.
3. When ready to cook, preheat the grill to high and line the grill pan with foil. Thread the vegetables and lamb on to eight metal kebab skewers; don't pack too tightly or they won't cook properly.
4. Grill the kebabs for a minute on each side, then lower the heat to moderate and cook for a further 5 minutes on each side or until well-browned and tender. Season with salt and pepper and serve with rice or warm pittas with a little extra yogurt for dipping.

Lamb Tagine

A classic from Morocco, the dish is slow-cooked until the meat is succulent and the sauce thick and almost syrupy. Fermented preserved lemons add a tangy contrast to the sweetness of the honey and prunes.

SERVES 4

30ml (2 tbsp) sunflower oil
750g (1¾lb) boneless shoulder of lamb, trimmed and cubed
2cm (¾in) piece fresh ginger, peeled and finely chopped
2 garlic cloves, peeled and crushed
pinch of saffron strands
10ml (2 tsp) ground cinnamon
about 300ml (½ pint) lamb or vegetable stock
200g (7oz) dried prunes, stones removed
15ml (1 tbsp) clear honey
salt and freshly ground black pepper
30ml (2 tbsp) chopped fresh herbs, e.g. mint, parsley or coriander
25g (1oz) Preserved Lemon rind (page 42), finely sliced
couscous, to serve

1. Heat the oil in a flameproof casserole or heavy-based saucepan, add the meat and fry for 2–3 minutes until browned. Turn down the heat as low as possible, add the ginger and garlic and stir for a further minute.
2. Add the saffron, cinnamon and enough stock to just cover the meat. Stir well, then cover and simmer very gently for 2 hours, adding a little more stock or water only if needed towards the end of cooking (the sauce should be thick). While the lamb cooks, put the prunes in a bowl, cover with cold water and leave to soak.
3. Drain the prunes and add to the lamb mixture with the honey. Season with salt and pepper. Bring back to the boil and simmer uncovered for a further 20–30 minutes or until the sauce is thick and well reduced.
4. Stir in the chopped herbs and serve scattered with finely sliced preserved lemon rind and accompanied by couscous.

Miso-glazed Halibut Steaks

This recipe is ideal for any firm-fleshed fish and works well with salmon, tuna and swordfish. If you have one, cook the fish in a ridged cast-iron grill pan, which makes attractive markings on the fish.

SERVES 4

For the glazed fish
4 halibut steaks, about 150g (5oz) each
30ml (2 tbsp) sunflower oil
10ml (2 tsp) brown miso paste
10ml (2 tsp) balsamic vinegar
10ml (2 tsp) dark soy sauce
5ml (1 tsp) smoked paprika

For the noodle salad
200g (7oz) dried rice noodles
15ml (1 tbsp) sunflower oil
2cm (¾in) piece fresh ginger, peeled and grated
1 red chilli, thinly sliced (seeds removed if preferred)
75g (3oz) mangetout, halved lengthways
150g (5oz) fresh beansprouts
2.5ml (½ tsp) brown miso paste
45ml (3 tbsp) hot (not boiling) water

1 For the glazed fish, place the halibut steaks in a shallow non-metallic dish. Mix together the oil, miso, vinegar, soy sauce and smoked paprika. Spoon over the fish steaks, turning them to coat both sides with the glaze mixture. Cover with cling film and leave to marinate in the fridge for at least 30 minutes, preferably longer and up to 12 hours.

2 Heat a lightly oiled ridged cast-iron grill pan or heavy-based frying pan over a high heat. Place the fish steaks in the pan and cook for 2–3 minutes on each side, basting occasionally, until the fish flakes easily.

3 For the noodle salad, cook the noodles in boiling water for 3 minutes, drain in a sieve and set aside. Heat the oil in a wok or large frying pan, add the ginger, chilli, mangetout and beansprouts. Stir-fry for 2 minutes, then turn off the heat and cover the pan with a lid. The vegetables will continue to cook a little in the steam.

4 Meanwhile, add the miso paste to the hot water in a small bowl and stir until blended. Remove the lid from the vegetable pan, add the noodles and cook for 1–2 minutes or until everything is hot and the vegetables are tender.

5 Pile the noodle mixture on to warmed plates. Drizzle over the blended miso, then place the fish steaks on top of the noodles. Serve straight away.

Tempeh Coconut Korma

This traditional southern Indian dish is usually very rich and made with double cream. Here, coconut yogurt is used to make the spicy sauce which coats a mixture of high-protein tempeh and vegetables to make a meal that will please vegetarians and meat-eaters alike.

SERVES 4

15ml (1 tbsp) coconut oil or ghee
1 onion, peeled and chopped
6 green cardamom pods
15ml (1 tbsp) coriander seeds
2.5ml (½ tsp) cumin seeds
10ml (2 tsp) ground turmeric
2 garlic cloves, peeled and crushed
2.5cm (1in) piece fresh ginger, peeled and grated
900g (2lb) mixed vegetables, e.g. cauliflower, carrots, potatoes, sweet potatoes and turnips, prepared and cut into 2cm (¾in) chunks
finely grated rind and juice of ½ lime or lemon
50g (2oz) ground almonds
300ml (½ pint) vegetable stock
225g (8oz) tempeh, cut into 2cm (¾in) chunks
5ml (1 tsp) cornflour
150ml (¼ pint) Coconut Yogurt (page 52)
salt and freshly ground black pepper
45ml (3 tbsp) chopped fresh coriander
Fermented Mango Preserve (page 45), to serve

1. Heat the coconut oil or ghee in a large heavy-based saucepan. Add the onion and gently cook for 10 minutes, stirring frequently until soft and just beginning to colour.
2. Meanwhile, remove the black seeds from the cardamom pods and finely grind with the coriander and cumin seeds in an electric grinder or using a pestle and mortar.

3 Sprinkle the ground spices and turmeric over the onion. Add the garlic and ginger and cook, stirring all the time, for a further minute. Add the vegetables to the pan with the citrus rind and juice, then sprinkle over the ground almonds. Stir well, then gradually stir in the stock. Cover and simmer over a gentle heat for 25 minutes.
4 Stir in the tempeh and cook for a further 5 minutes or until the vegetables are tender. Put the cornflour in a bowl and stir in a little of the yogurt to blend. Stir in the remaining yogurt.
5 Stir the yogurt mixture, a large spoonful at a time, into the vegetable mixture. Season to taste with salt and pepper and gently cook for a few minutes until just starting to bubble again. Sprinkle with chopped coriander and serve with fermented mango preserve.

Notes
- Stirring a little cornflour into the yogurt will stabilise it and stop the sauce curdling.
- Tempeh has been enjoyed in Indonesia for over two thousand years. It is made by culturing partially cooked soya beans with *Rhizopus oligosporus* mould to produce a nutty flavour and a texture similar to mushrooms. Unlike other fermented foods tempeh must be cooked and is usually served in thick slices. As well as being high in protein, it is a great source of vitamin B12, which is often lacking in vegetarian and vegan diets.

Tempeh Veggie-burgers

Tempeh is a fantastic food for those on a meat-free diet and here it is combined with grated courgette to make moist vegetarian burgers. Serve between slices of ciabatta and top with probiotic tomato ketchup, or accompany with spicy fermented vegetables such as pickled radishes.

SERVES 4

15ml (1 tbsp) coconut or sunflower oil, plus extra for frying
1 red onion, peeled and finely chopped
1 medium courgette, about 100g (4oz), trimmed and grated
225g (8oz) tempeh
30ml (2 tbsp) chopped fresh parsley
salt and freshly ground black pepper
8 slices Ciabatta (page 90)
salad leaves, mayonnaise or Probiotic Tomato Ketchup (page 43) or Pickled Radishes with Red Onion and Apple (page 32), to serve

1. Heat 15ml (1 tbsp) of the oil in a frying pan and gently cook the onion for 5 minutes, stirring frequently. Add the courgette and cook for a further 2–3 minutes or until just tender. Leave to cool.
2. Break up the tempeh into smaller pieces and put in a food processor. Pulse for a few seconds until finely chopped, then add the onion and courgette mixture and process for about 15 seconds until very finely chopped. Add the parsley, season with salt and pepper and process for a further 15 seconds or until everything is mixed together.
3. Divide the mixture into four equal portions and shape into oval burgers, about 2cm (¾in) thick and roughly the same size and shape as the ciabatta slices.
4. Heat the remaining 15ml (1 tbsp) of oil in a large heavy-based non-stick frying pan and cook the burgers over a medium heat for about 3 minutes on each side, until lightly browned.
5. Serve the burgers hot between two slices of ciabatta, adding salad leaves, mayonnaise, ketchup or pickles to your liking.

Japanese Red Rice with Natto

This dish contains a combination of aduki beans and natto, a Japanese fermented food. Flavoured with spring onions and ginger, the sticky rice is cooked in the liquid from the beans, giving it a reddish hue.

SERVES 4

200g (7oz) glutinous rice
200g (7oz) can aduki beans
5ml (1 tsp) sesame oil
4 spring onions, finely sliced
2.5cm (1in) piece fresh ginger, peeled and grated
pinch of salt
180g (6oz) packet natto
10ml (2 tsp) toasted sesame seeds

1. Rinse the rice under cold running water until the water runs clear, then drain well. Put in a bowl, cover with cold water and leave to soak for 1 hour.
2. Drain the aduki beans, reserving the red liquid. Heat the oil in a pan and gently fry the spring onions for 2 minutes. Add the ginger and cook for a few more seconds.
3. Drain the rice and put in a measuring jug with the drained beans. Add an equal quantity of liquid, using the liquid from the bean can, topped up with cold water as needed. Tip into the pan, gently stir and bring to the boil.
4. Season with a little salt (not too much as the natto is salty) and lower the heat to a gentle simmer. Part-cover with a lid and cook for about 15 minutes or until most of the liquid has been absorbed.
5. Place the natto on top of the rice, cover with the pan lid and leave the rice to steam undisturbed for a further 10 minutes. Use a fork to break up the softened natto and gently mix into the rice. Serve straight away, scattered with sesame seeds.

Notes
- Natto is made from fermented soya beans and in Japan is often eaten for breakfast with rice. It has a strong pungent smell, similar to the ammonic whiff of very over-ripe Camembert cheese, and a gooey texture (the beans are held together with long stretchy strings of slime). As such, it is an acquired taste for most Westerners. It is made by steaming natto soya beans and then fermenting with the beneficial bacteria, *Bacillus subtilis*. Nutritionally, natto has much to offer: it is exceptionally high in protein, vitamins B and K and calcium. Natto contains an enzyme known as nattokinase which has anti-inflammatory health benefits and is used to prevent and treat blood clots: it works by breaking down fibrin, a protein that in excess contributes to heart disease and strokes.
- Glutinous rice, sometimes referred to as 'Chinese rice' or 'sticky rice' is widely used in South-east Asian cooking. The almost round grains stick together after cooking, making it easy to roll into balls or eat with chopsticks. The name is slightly misleading as like all rice, it contains no gluten. Glutinous rice can be bought in Asian stores or via the Internet.

DESSERTS

Sourdough Pancakes

When making a sourdough loaf there is usually a small amount of leftover pre-ferment or easy sourdough starter that you can use to start another loaf. If you don't want to make more bread, it can also be used to make these light and fluffy pancakes.

SERVES 4

65g (2½oz) plain white or spelt flour
pinch of salt
2 eggs
75g (3oz) Pre-ferment (page 84–5) or Easy Sourdough Starter (page 87)
150ml (¼ pint) milk
oil for frying
Cultured Butter (page 57) or freshly squeezed lemon juice and pure maple syrup, agave or honey, to serve

1. Sift the flour and salt into a mixing bowl. Make a hollow in the middle and break in the eggs. Whisk the eggs together with a fork, then add the pre-ferment or sourdough starter.
2. Gradually beat in the milk, drawing in the flour from the sides to make a smooth batter. Cover and leave to stand for 20 minutes.
3. Heat the minimum of oil in an 18cm (7in) heavy-based frying pan and pour in just enough batter to cover the base of the pan. Cook over a moderately high heat for about 1 minute until golden brown, then turn or toss the pancake and cook the second side for about 45 seconds.
4. Transfer the pancake to a plate and keep hot. Repeat with the remaining batter, adding a little more oil to the pan when needed. Serve as soon as all the pancakes are cooked, with a little cultured butter, or sprinkled with freshly squeezed lemon juice and drizzled with maple syrup, agave or honey, if liked.

Buttermilk Panna Cotta

The traditional recipe for panna cotta from the Piedmont region of Italy is made entirely with double cream. This lighter version has a blend of buttermilk and cream. It still has a velvety smooth creamy texture, but is much lower in fat. It's delicious served with chopped fresh fruit or fruit compote.

SERVES 4

500ml (17fl oz) Buttermilk (page 57) or a mixture of buttermilk and semi-skimmed milk
15ml (1 tbsp) powdered gelatine
65g (2½oz) golden caster sugar
thinly pared strip of orange rind
100ml (4fl oz) double cream
5ml (1 tsp) pure vanilla paste or vanilla extract

1. Pour 150ml (¼ pint) of the buttermilk into a saucepan. Sprinkle over the gelatine and leave to soak for 5 minutes, until spongy.
2. Add the sugar and orange rind. Gently heat, without boiling, stirring until the gelatine and sugar have completely dissolved. (Take care as overheating the gelatine will stop it from setting.) Remove from the heat and leave to cool and infuse for 5 minutes.
3. Remove the strip of orange rind, then stir in the cream, the rest of the buttermilk and the vanilla. Pour into four moulds or ramekins, each with a capacity of about 175ml (6fl oz). Chill for at least 2 hours or until set.
4. To serve, dip the moulds or ramekins into hot water for a few seconds. Place an inverted serving plate over the top of each, then turn upside down, holding the two firmly together. Lift off the mould or ramekin. Serve with fresh fruit.

Berry Frozen Yogurt

This is an 'instant' dessert that you can create in a couple of minutes without the need for lengthy churning in an ice-cream maker. Choose a frozen berry mixture with a high proportion of 'sweet' fruits such as strawberries and raspberries and not too many blackcurrants or redcurrants, which can be very tart without the addition of sugar or sweetener. This is a great way to use up a glut of home-grown berries frozen at their peak to enjoy later in the year.

SERVES 4

250g (9oz) chilled whole milk Greek Yogurt (page 50)
250g (9oz) frozen mixed berries
15ml (1 tbsp) honey or agave, plus extra to serve

1. Put all the ingredients in a food processor and pulse-blend for about 30 seconds or until fairly smooth and the mixture comes together in the texture of a slightly softened ice cream.
2. Spoon into chilled bowls and serve straight away. If liked, drizzle with extra honey or agave and sprinkle over a few toasted chopped nuts.

Note
If time allows, chill the yogurt in the freezer for 20 minutes before making. You can also put the frozen yogurt in the freezer for up to 30 minutes before eating (if, for example you want to make before serving a main course), but don't leave for much longer or it will become too hard and icy.

Fresh Fruit Jelly

Although you need to plan in advance as this takes several hours to set, this is a really quick and easy dessert. This is a great way to introduce children to fermented fruit juice and is popular with adults too.

SERVES 4

600ml (1 pint) Sparkling Orange Juice (page 80)
20ml (4 tsp) powdered gelatine
2 oranges
100g (4oz) seedless black or white grapes, preferably organic

1. Spoon 75ml (5 tbsp) of sparkling orange juice into a small heatproof bowl, then sprinkle over the gelatine. Leave to soak for 5 minutes until the gelatine has absorbed all the juice and looks spongy.
2. Place the bowl in a pan of near-boiling water and leave for a few minutes, then stir until the gelatine has dissolved. Remove the bowl from the pan and leave to cool for 5 minutes.
3. Meanwhile, peel the oranges with a sharp knife, removing all the white pith, then cut into segments between the membranes, catching any juices in a bowl. Divide the orange segments and grapes between four individual serving dishes or glasses.
4. Stir the gelatine mixture into the rest of the sparkling orange juice and divide between the dishes. Chill in the fridge for at least 2 hours or until set.

Note
Small children can choke on whole grapes; cut them into quarters if using large grapes, if using smaller grapes, cut them in half.

Variation
You can decorate the jellies with swirls of 'yogurt cream' if liked: Sprinkle 10ml (2 tsp) powdered gelatine over 45ml (3 tbsp) cold water in a small bowl and leave to soak for 5 minutes. Place the bowl in a pan of near-boiling water and stir until the gelatine has dissolved. Leave to cool for 5 minutes. Mix together 300ml (½ pint) Greek Yogurt (page 50), 15ml (1 tbsp) fructose and 5ml (1 tsp) vanilla extract. Stir in the gelatine mixture and chill in the fridge for 30 minutes, until beginning to set around the edges. Whisk 1 egg white until stiff (use a pasteurised egg white from a carton or reconstituted egg white powder, if serving to young children) and carefully fold into the yogurt mixture. Spoon into a piping bag fitted with a large fluted nozzle and pipe swirls on top of the jellies.

Coconut Kefir Cheesecake

Coconut kefir cheese has an intense coconut flavour and rich creamy texture. This is not too sweet and thinner than a deep American-style cheesecake. It is especially good served with juicy ripe fruit such as diced mangoes or with strawberries or raspberries when in season.

SERVES 6–8

For the base
100g (4oz) skinned hazelnuts, preferably toasted (ready-chopped ones are fine)
50g (2oz) shelled Brazil nuts
150g (5oz) dried dates, roughly chopped
40g (1½oz) raw coconut oil

For the topping
350g (12oz) coconut Kefir Soft Cheese (page 66)
5ml (1 tsp) vanilla extract
15ml (1 tbsp) clear honey

1. Line the base of a 20cm (8in) round loose-bottomed cake tin or spring-clip tin with baking parchment. With the motor running, pour the nuts into a food processor and process until roughly chopped. Add the dates and continue blending until finely chopped but not pureed; the mixture should look like fine breadcrumbs.
2. Gently melt the coconut oil in a saucepan (in hot weather it will already be liquid, so this won't be necessary). Add the chopped nuts and dates and stir until combined. Spoon into the tin and press down with the back of a spoon to smooth and level. Chill in the fridge while making the topping.

3 For the topping, beat the coconut kefir cheese, vanilla and honey together (the mixture will be very soft at this stage). Spoon on top of the base and spread out evenly. Cover the top of the tin with cling film and chill for at least 2 hours until firm.
4 Run a round-bladed knife around the edge of the tin, then push up the base to unmould the cheesecake. Transfer to a plate. If the topping is still a little soft for slicing, firm up by placing in the freezer for half an hour. Serve each slice drizzled with a little more honey, if liked, or with chopped fresh fruit.

Variations
- You can also make this with unsalted dairy milk kefir cheese.
- If liked, flavour the base with the finely grated rind of ½ unwaxed lime or with 2.5ml (½ tsp) ground cinnamon.

Chocolate and Avocado Mousse

This is an intensely chocolatey mousse. Although avocado may sound strange in a dessert it gives a rich creamy texture without the need for eggs or dairy.

SERVES 4-6

75g (3oz) dark chocolate with a high cocoa content (at least 70%)
60ml (4 tbsp) maple syrup
10ml (2 tsp) vanilla extract
tiny pinch of salt
75ml (5 tbsp) Coconut Milk Kefir (page 64)
30ml (2 tbsp) cocoa powder, sieved
2 small ripe avocados
Crème Fraiche (page 56), chocolate curls or cocoa powder, to serve (optional)

1. Break the chocolate into squares and put in a heatproof bowl over a pan of very hot (not boiling) water. Leave for 2–3 minutes, then stir until melted. Remove the bowl from the heat.
2. Stir the maple syrup into the melted chocolate, followed by the vanilla, salt, coconut milk kefir and cocoa powder.
3. Halve, stone and remove the skins from the avocados. Roughly chop and put in a food processor. Add the chocolate mixture, then blend until smooth and silky.
4. Spoon into four or six serving glasses or ramekins and chill for at least 3 hours before serving. If liked, decorate with a small dollop of crème fraiche and some chocolate curls or a very light dusting of cocoa powder.

Variation
You can make these with milk kefir if preferred (although the mousses will no longer be dairy-free).

Tropical Fruit Salad

This simple fruit salad with golden and orange-coloured fruits looks stunning served in a large glass bowl. Translucent cubes of nata de coco add a subtle coconut flavour and texture, and rejuvelac adds a slight lemony flavour to the fragrant fruit syrup.

SERVES 4

1 large ripe papaya
2 large ripe mangoes
4 ripe passionfruit
340g (12oz) jar nata de coco (see Note)
60ml (4 tbsp) Rejuvelac (page 77)

1. Halve the papaya lengthways and scoop out the black seeds with a teaspoon. Peel the fruit and cut into 2cm (¾in) cubes. Prepare the mangoes by cutting lengthways on either side of the stone. Peel and cut the flesh into 2cm (¾in) cubes. Put the fruit in a serving bowl.
2. Scoop the pulp of each passionfruit into a small saucepan. Add 60ml (4 tbsp) of syrup from the jar of nata de coco. Heat gently until warm, then press the mixture through a sieve over the bowl of fruit and pour over the rejuvelac.
3. Drain the nata de coco and add to the bowl. Gently mix everything together. Scatter the passionfruit seeds over the top and serve lightly chilled.

Note
Nata de coco (meaning 'cream of coconut' in Spanish) is a translucent jelly, usually sold cut into small cubes. It is made by fermenting coconut water, during which process the gel is formed through the natural production of microbial cellulose.

BAKES AND CAKES

Simple Soda Bread

This is an excellent alternative to fermented and yeasted breads when you need a loaf in a hurry as it only takes minutes to make, using either home-made or shop-bought buttermilk. It is delicious served warm, and stales quickly, so bake and serve on the same day.

MAKES 1 LOAF

350g (12oz) wholemeal plain flour
100g (4oz) pinhead oatmeal
10ml (2 tsp) bicarbonate of soda
5ml (1 tsp) salt
300ml (½ pint) Buttermilk (page 57)
30ml (2 tbsp) milk, plus extra for brushing
10ml (2 tsp) clear honey
Cultured Butter (page 57), to serve (optional)

1. Preheat the oven to 200°C (fan 180°C), gas 6. Put the flour, oatmeal, bicarbonate of soda and salt in a mixing bowl and stir until well mixed. Make a hollow in the middle of the dry ingredients.
2. Stir the buttermilk, milk and honey together in a jug. Pour into the hollow and mix to a soft dough. Turn out on to a lightly floured surface and knead for a minute or two until smooth.

3 Shape the dough into a round about 20cm (8in) across and place on a lightly greased baking sheet. Using a sharp knife, cut a deep cross on top of the dough.
4 Brush the top with milk and bake for 30–35 minutes or until risen and the loaf sounds hollow when tapped underneath. Cool on a wire rack and serve barely warm or cold in thick slices. Spread with cultured butter, if liked.

Brown Buttermilk Scones

Buttermilk makes the lightest scones as its slight acidity combined with self-raising flour helps them rise without the after-taste that adding extra bicarbonate of soda or baking powder can leave. Although the beneficial bacteria won't survive the high oven temperature, this is an excellent way to use up leftover buttermilk when making cultured butter.

MAKES 6-8

100g (4oz) wholemeal self-raising flour, preferably organic
100g (4oz) white self-raising flour, preferably organic
1.5ml (¼ tsp) salt
50g (2oz) chilled butter, cut into small cubes
25g (1oz) golden caster sugar
200ml (7fl oz) Buttermilk (page 57)
Cultured Butter (page 57), to serve (optional)

1. Preheat the oven to 220°C (fan 200°C), gas 7. Lightly grease a baking sheet or line with baking parchment.
2. Sift the flours and salt into a mixing bowl, adding the bran left in the sieve. Add the butter, then rub together with your fingertips and thumbs until the mixture resembles coarse breadcrumbs; it will be lighter if there are still some small flakes of butter, so don't over-rub.
3. Stir in the sugar. Make a hollow in the flour mixture. Reserve 15ml (1 tbsp) of the buttermilk for glazing, then add the rest to the hollow. Mix to a soft, sticky dough.

4 Knead on a lightly floured surface for a few seconds until smooth, but don't over-work the dough. Pat the dough gently with your hands or lightly roll with a rolling pin until the dough is 2cm (¾in) thick and then cut into rounds with a 5–6cm (2–2½in) cutter.
5 Place on the baking sheet and brush the tops with the reserved buttermilk. Bake for 10–12 minutes, until well-risen and golden brown. Transfer to a wire rack to cool. Serve warm with cultured butter, if liked.

> **Note**
> You can make the scones with cultured rather than ordinary butter, but the beneficial bacteria will be destroyed by the high oven temperature.

Creamy Kefir Carrot Cake

This is a raw, vegan and gluten-free version of the ever-popular baked carrot cake, with kefir providing that lovely slightly tangy taste of the usual cream-cheese frosting. You will need a powerful blender to make the cashew nut topping smooth and creamy.

MAKES 12 PORTIONS

For the topping
200g (7oz) cashew nuts
filtered water
3 Medjool or soft dates, stones removed
150ml (¼ pint) Milk Kefir (page 62)
7.5ml (1½ tsp) vanilla extract

For the base
finely grated rind of ½ unwaxed orange
175g (6oz) porridge oats
50g (2oz) ground, chopped or whole nuts (preferably lightly toasted if chopped or whole), e.g. almonds, Brazil nuts or walnuts
10ml (2 tsp) ground cinnamon
5ml (1 tsp) ground ginger
175g (6oz) carrots, preferably organic, coarsely grated
100g (4oz) Medjool or soft dates, stones removed
50g (2oz) walnut pieces, to decorate

1. Put the cashew nuts in a glass, ceramic or stainless steel bowl and pour over enough filtered water to cover by about 5cm (2in). Leave to soak for 8 hours or overnight (in hot weather, put the bowl in the fridge). If you want to speed up soaking time, put the nuts in a heatproof bowl, cover with boiling water and leave to soak for 4 hours.
2. Drain and rinse the nuts, then return the nuts to the bowl, add the dates, then pour over the kefir. Stir to coat the nuts and dates and leave to soak briefly while making the base.

3 For the base, line a loose-bottomed 20cm (8in) square or 23cm (9in) round tin with baking parchment. Lightly grease the tin with sunflower oil. Put the orange rind and oats in a food processor. Add the nuts if using whole ones and blend until coarsely ground.
4 Add the nuts if using ground ones, cinnamon and ginger and blend for a few more seconds to mix, then add the carrots and dates and blend until completely mixed. Spread the mixture over the base of the lined tin and level with the back of a spoon. Chill in the fridge while making the topping.
5 Using a slotted spoon, transfer the soaked cashew nuts and dates into a powerful blender or food processor retaining the kefir. Add the vanilla and pulse until finely chopped. With the motor running, slowly pour in the kefir, stopping now and then to scrape down the sides. Blend until the mixture is smooth and creamy.
6 Spoon and spread the topping over the base, levelling with the back of the spoon. Sprinkle over the walnut pieces. Chill in the fridge for 2–3 hours or until very firm. Remove the cake from the tin and cut into portions.

Note
If the topping is too soft to slice easily, pop the cake into the freezer for about 30 minutes before cutting into pieces.

Variation
You can substitute the grated carrot with 50g (2oz) Carrot Kraut with Ginger and Orange (page 41) when making the base (drain it well). Its slightly salty flavour works well here.

Yogurt Cake with Lemon and Pistachios

This Moroccan cake has a delicate and moist spongy texture and can be eaten warm or chilled. Serve as a dessert with a generous spoonful of crème fraiche, or with your mid-morning coffee.

SERVES 6-8

3 medium eggs, at room temperature, separated
75g (3oz) golden caster sugar
5ml (1 tsp) vanilla extract
15ml (1 tbsp) plain flour
300ml (½ pint) Greek Yogurt (page 50)
finely grated rind and juice of 1 unwaxed lemon
50g (2oz) unsalted pistachio nuts, roughly chopped
Crème Fraiche (page 56), to serve

1. Preheat the oven to 180°C (fan 160°C), gas 4. Lightly grease a 23–25cm (9–10in) round tin (not a loose-bottomed tin) and line the base with baking parchment.
2. Beat the egg yolks, 50g (2oz) of the sugar and the vanilla in a bowl until pale and fluffy. In a separate bowl, whisk the egg whites with the remaining 25g (1oz) sugar until soft peaks form.
3. Sift the flour over the egg yolk mixture, then add the yogurt, lemon rind and juice and half the pistachios. Gently fold in until almost mixed. Add the egg white mixture and continue folding until just mixed. Spoon the mixture into the prepared tin.
4. Place the tin in a roasting dish and pour enough hot (not boiling) water into the roasting dish to come about halfway up the cake tin. Bake for 20 minutes, then sprinkle the remaining pistachios over the top and bake for a further 15–20 minutes or until the cake is firm and lightly browned on top.
5. Remove the cake from the roasting tin and leave for 20 minutes, then carefully turn out and serve warm or leave to cool and chill before serving with crème fraiche.

SIX SUPER SMOOTHIES

Packed with healthy ingredients, smoothies and blends are an easy way to get a portion of fermented food, and count as at least two of the daily recommended five to seven portions of fruit and vegetables. They are particularly useful for those times when you have been too hectic to eat properly.

Breakfast Blend

A great way to start the day, this smoothie is ideal for breakfast as it is quick and nourishing, containing a good balance of protein, antioxidant vitamins, and minerals such as calcium, potassium and iron.

SERVES 1

1 small ripe banana
small handful of kale, about 15g (½oz)
50g (2oz) fresh or frozen blueberries
5ml (1 tsp) wheat germ
100ml (4fl oz) plain yogurt (page 49)
150ml (¼ pint) chilled skimmed milk

1 Peel and slice the banana. Wash the kale if necessary and shake dry, removing any large, tough stems. Put the banana and kale in the blender with the blueberries, wheat germ, yogurt and milk.
2 Pulse the blender for a few seconds until the fruit and kale are finely chopped, then blend for about 30 seconds until smooth. Check the consistency; add a little more milk if you prefer a thinner smoothie and briefly blend again.

Mango and Orange Wake-up

This invigorating drink should ideally be made with fresh orange juice. It tastes better than shop-bought juice and is better for you, too, as even cartons of 'freshly squeezed' juice gradually lose their vitamin C content once opened.

SERVES 2

1 medium ripe mango
1 small ripe banana
1 large orange
100ml (4fl oz) Water Kefir (page 70)
10ml (2 tsp) camu-camu powder (optional, see Note)

1. Cut a lengthways slice on either side of the mango stone, then peel away the skin and chop the flesh from around the stone. Peel and slice the banana. Halve the orange and squeeze out the juice.
2. Put the mango, banana and orange juice in a blender. Add the water kefir and camu-camu powder, if using. Pulse the blender for a few seconds until the fruit is finely chopped, then blend for about 45 seconds, until the mixture is smooth. Pour over ice cubes into two glasses.

Note
Camu-camu is a light brown powder made by drying and grinding the purplish-red berry-like camu-camu fruit which grow in South America. Anti-viral and anti-inflammatory, it is a good source of vitamin C and the flavour has a hint of caramel.

Blueberry Brain Booster

Antioxidants in blueberries stimulate the flow of blood and oxygen to the brain and can help to boost concentration and memory for up to five hours after consumption. Drink this at breakfast or lunchtime and it should help keep you from flagging in the afternoon.

SERVES 1

100g (4oz) fresh or frozen blueberries
pinch of ground cinnamon
2 Brazil nuts
250ml (8fl oz) Coconut Milk Kefir (page 64)
5ml (1 tsp) goji berry powder (optional)

1. Wash the blueberries if using fresh, then put in a blender with the cinnamon, nuts and coconut milk kefir. Add the goji berry powder, if using.
2. Pulse the blender for a few seconds until the blueberries and nuts are finely chopped, then blend for about 1 minute, or until the mixture is very smooth.

Note
Goji berries have been used in traditional Chinese medicine for many centuries and in recent decades they have been acclaimed in the West as a 'superfood'. They are believed to improve immunity and brain power and protect against cardiovascular disease. Buy them in health-food shops and larger supermarkets.

Pistachio and Almond Lassi

In India, lassi comes in many flavours, but spices and nuts are especially popular. All unsalted nuts can help to reduce cholesterol levels and cut the risk of type 2 diabetes and cardiovascular disease, but pistachios are particularly effective. Rejuvelac has a slightly tart lemony flavour and works well in this refreshing drink.

SERVES 1

50g (2oz) shelled unsalted pistachio nuts
25g (1oz) blanched almonds
150ml (¼ pint) chilled Rejuvelac (page 77)
5ml (1 tsp) lecithin granules (optional, see Note)
100ml (4fl oz) plain yogurt (page 49)
ice cubes or crushed ice, to serve

1. Put the nuts in a bowl and pour over enough cold filtered water to cover them by about 5cm (2in). Leave to soak at room temperature for 6 hours, or overnight in the fridge.
2. Drain the nuts and put them in a blender. Add the chilled rejuvelac and lecithin, if using. Pulse the blender for a few seconds, then blend for about 45 seconds until fairly smooth. Add the yogurt and blend for a further 30 seconds. Pour into a glass and serve with ice.

Note
Creamy-beige lecithin granules are derived from soya beans and act as a thickener and emulsifier, helping to prevent blends from separating. Lecithin plays an important role in fat metabolism and helps the body break down and dispose of low-density lipoprotein (LDL) cholesterol.

Summer Fruit Sipper

Fluid intake is important, especially during the hot summer months. Chilled kombucha makes a great base for this thirst-quenching smoothie.

SERVES 1

1 large wedge of watermelon, or ½ a 'baby' watermelon, about 250g (9oz) flesh in total
50g (2oz) fresh or frozen strawberries
250ml (8fl oz) chilled Kombucha (page 73)
fresh mint leaves (optional)

1 Cut the watermelon flesh into chunks, discarding any large hard pips. Wash the strawberries, if using fresh, and hull them. Put the watermelon and strawberries in a blender and pour in the chilled kombucha.
2 Pulse the blender for a few seconds until the fruit is finely chopped, then blend for about 30 seconds until smooth. Add a few fresh mint leaves if liked, then blend again until they are finely chopped and the drink has a speckled appearance.

Avocado, Coconut and Pear Smoothie

Coconut water kefir makes a fantastic base for a dairy-free smoothie. Although avocados have a high fat content, it is monounsaturated fat, so it can help to lower blood cholesterol levels.

SERVES 2

1 small or medium ripe avocado
10ml (2 tsp) lime juice
1 ripe pear
175ml (6fl oz) Coconut Water Kefir (page 72)

1 Cut the avocado in half and remove the stone. Scoop out the flesh and put in the blender, then sprinkle over the lime juice. Wash the pear (or peel off the skin if you prefer), cut into quarters and remove the core. Roughly chop and add to the blender with the coconut water kefir.
2 Pulse the blender for a few seconds until the avocado and pear are finely chopped, then blend for about 45 seconds or until the mixture is smooth. Divide between two glasses.

Index

aduki beans: Japanese Red Rice with Natto 139–40
almonds
   Fermented Mango Preserve 45
   Pistachio and Almond Lassi 160
   Smoked Aubergine and Yogurt Dip 106
   Tempeh Coconut Korma 136–7
Alzheimer's 8
anti-nutrients 4
apples 19
   Marinated Herring and Beetroot Salad 110
   Pickled Radishes with Red Onion and Apple 32–3
   Spiced Red Cabbage and Apple Sauerkraut 25
asparagus: Griddled Asparagus with Yogurt Hollandaise 104
aubergines
   Mediterranean Lamb Kebabs 132
   Smoked Aubergine and Yogurt Dip 106
autoimmune conditions 5, 8
avocados
   Avocado, Coconut and Pear Smoothie 162
   Chocolate and Avocado Mousse 148
   Smoked Salmon and Pasta Salad with Avocado Kefir Dressing 111

B vitamins 2, 4, 49, 77, 137
bacteria 1, 2, 3, 4, 7, 8, 9, 12, 14, 15, 20, 49
bacterial infections 1–2, 6
bananas
   Breakfast Blend 157
   Mango and Orange Wake-up 158
beef
   Hunter's Stew 128–9
   Noodles in Chilled Beef Broth 96–8
beetroots 19
   Beetroot Kvass 79
   Borscht 102
   Marinated Herring and Beetroot Salad 110
   Pickled Beetroot and Turnips 40
blueberries
   Blueberry Brain Booster 159
   Breakfast Blend 157
bowls 14–15
breads 83–93
   California Sourdough 88–9
   Italian Ciabatta 90–1
   Landbrot 92–3
   Simple Soda Bread 150–1
   Sourdough Loaf 84–6
brine 9, 10, 17
broad beans: Minted Pea and Broad Bean Soup with Yogurt 101
Butter, Cultured 57–8
Buttermilk 57–8
   Brown Buttermilk Scones 152–3
   Buttermilk Panna Cotta 142
   Simple Soda Bread 150–1

cabbage 19
   Borscht 102
   Fermented Spring Vegetables 30
   Mixed Vegetable Slaw 26–7
   Simple Sauerkraut 23–4
   Spiced Red Cabbage and Apple Sauerkraut 25
   see also Chinese leaves
cakes and scones
   Brown Buttermilk Scones 152–3
   Creamy Kefir Carrot Cake 154–5
   Yogurt Cake with Lemon and Pistachios 156
calcium 4, 49
camu-camu 158
caraway seeds 21
carrots 19
   Carrot Kraut with Ginger and Orange 41

Cauliflower, Carrot and Pepper Pickles 31
Classic Kimchi 34–5
Creamy Kefir Carrot Cake 154–5
Fermented Spring Vegetables 30
Mixed Vegetable Slaw 26–7
Tempeh Coconut Korma 136–7
cauliflower
  Cauliflower, Carrot and Pepper Pickles 31
  Tempeh Coconut Korma 136–7
cheese
  Blue Cheese Dip 121
  Coconut Kefir Cheesecake 146–7
  Creamy Seafood Wraps with Kimchi 125
  Fresh Tomato and Kefir Cheese Bruschetta 116–17
  Kefir Soft Cheese 66
  Labneh 51
  Mango-stuffed Chicken Breasts 126–7
chicken
  Chicken Miso Soup 99–100
  Mango-stuffed Chicken Breasts 126–7
  Sesame Chicken Salad 120–1
  Summer Chicken Caesar Salad 112–13
  Yogurt-spiced Chicken Skewers 108
chickpeas
  Couscous and Grilled Pepper Salad with Labneh 118–19
  Creamy Hummus 107
  Quinoa Falafels in Wholemeal Pittas with Mixed Vegetable Slaw 122–4
Chinese leaves
  Chunky Kimchi 36–7
  Classic Kimchi 34–5
  White Kimchi 38–9
Chocolate and Avocado Mousse 148
cholesterol 160
chopping boards 15
coconut
  Coconut Drinking Yogurt 7, 54
  Coconut Milk Kefir 6, 64–5
  Coconut Water Kefir 72
  Coconut Yogurt 6, 52–3
  creamed coconut 53
  nata de coco 149
  Tempeh Coconut Korma 136–7
coeliac disease 5

colanders 14
constipation 5
courgettes 19
  Fermented Spring Vegetables 30
  Mediterranean Lamb Kebabs 132
  Summer Chicken Caesar Salad 112–13
  Tempeh Veggie-burgers 138
Couscous and Grilled Pepper Salad with Labneh 118–19
crème fraiche 56, 58
Crohn's disease 5–6
cucumbers 19
  Dill Pickles 28–9
  Smoked Salmon and Pasta Salad with Avocado Kefir Dressing 111
  Tzatziki 105

dairy foods and dairy alternatives 47–67
dates
  Coconut Kefir Cheesecake 146–7
  Creamy Kefir Carrot Cake 154–5
desserts
  Berry Frozen Yogurt 143
  Buttermilk Panna Cotta 142
  Chocolate and Avocado Mousse 148
  Coconut Kefir Cheesecake 146–7
  Fresh Fruit Jelly 144–5
  Sourdough Pancakes 141
  Tropical Fruit Salad 149
detoxification 74
diarrhoea 5, 6, 7
digestive disorders 4, 5–8
dill 21
  Dill Pickles 28–9
dried fruit
  Fermented Mango Preserve 45
  Water Kefir 70–1
drinks 69–81
  Beetroot Kvass 79
  Buttermilk 57–8
  Coconut Drinking Yogurt 54
  Coconut Milk Kefir 64–5
  Coconut Water Kefir 72
  Kombucha 73–6
  Milk Kefir 62–3
  Probiotic Limeade 81

Rejuvelac 77–8
Sparkling Orange Juice 80
Water Kefir 70–1
see also smoothies
dysbiosis 2

eggs
Noodles in Chilled Beef Broth 96–8
Thai-style Vegetable Omelette 103
equipment 12–16
sterilising 15–16, 17

fermentation crocks 13
fermented foods
basic ingredients 8–12
digestibility 3
equipment 12–16
health benefits 1, 4, 5–8
including in your diet 18
laxative effects 5, 6, 18
nutritional benefits 3–4
origins 1, 47
safe fermenting 17–18
fish and seafood
Creamy Seafood Wraps with Kimchi 125
Marinated Herring and Beetroot Salad 110
Miso-glazed Halibut Steaks 134–5
Summer Chicken Caesar Salad 112–13
see also smoked salmon
food poisoning 6, 17
food preservation methods 3
fruit
fermenting 19–22
see also individual index entries

gastro-related problems 5–8
gastroenteritis 6
gluten intolerance 5
gochugaru (Korean chilli powder) 35
goji berries 159
gut bacteria 1, 2, 3, 4, 8, 17

immune system disorders 4, 5
immune system support 1, 4
inflammatory bowel disease (IBD) 6
irritable bowel syndrome (IBS) 6

jars and crocks 12–13
airlock jars 12
fermenting crocks 13
jars, filling 18
sealing 18
juniper berries 21

kale
Breakfast Blend 157
Fermented Spring Vegetables 30
kefir 3, 21, 47
Avocado, Coconut and Pear Smoothie 162
Blueberry Brain Booster 159
Chocolate and Avocado Mousse 148
Coconut Kefir Cheesecake 146–7
Coconut Milk Kefir 64–5
Coconut Water Kefir 72
Creamy Hummus 107
Creamy Kefir Carrot Cake 154–5
Fresh Tomato and Kefir Cheese Bruschetta 116–17
Kefir Cream 67
Kefir Ranch-style Dip 109
Kefir Soft Cheese 66
Mango and Orange Wake-up 158
Milk Kefir 62–3
milk kefir grains 59, 60–1
powdered starter culture 59
Ranch-style Dressing 113
Smoked Salmon and Pasta Salad with Avocado Kefir Dressing 111
Water Kefir 6, 11, 70–1
kimchi 19
Chunky Kimchi 36–7
Classic Kimchi 34–5
Creamy Seafood Wraps with Kimchi 125
Noodles in Chilled Beef Broth 96–8
Salmon and Kimchi Sushi Rolls 114–15
Thai-style Vegetable Omelette 103
White Kimchi 38–9
kohlrabi 19
Kombucha 73–6
Summer Fruit Sipper 161

Labneh 51

Couscous and Grilled Pepper Salad
    with Labneh 118–19
lactase 7
lactic acid 3, 48, 49
lacto-fermentation 3
Lactobacillus acidophilus 7
Lactobacillus bulgaricus 1
lactose intolerance 3, 7
lamb
    Lamb Tagine 133
    Mediterranean Lamb Kebabs 132
laxative effect 5, 6, 18
leaky gut syndrome 7
lecithin 160
leeks: White Kimchi 38–9
lemons
    Lamb Tagine 133
    Preserved Lemons 42
    Yogurt Cake with Lemon and
        Pistachios 156
limes: Probiotic Limeade 81
lycopene 43

mangoes
    Fermented Mango Preserve 45
    Mango-stuffed Chicken Breasts 126–7
    Tropical Fruit Salad 149
Metchnikoff, Dr Élie 1
mezze
    Creamy Hummus 107
    Kefir Ranch-style Dip 109
    Smoked Aubergine and Yogurt Dip 106
    Tzatziki 105
    Yogurt-spiced Chicken Skewers 108
microbes 1, 3, 11
milk
    cows' milk 60
    goats' milk 60
    lactose-free milk 61
    raw milk 60–1
    sheep's milk 60
milk products, fermented *see* dairy foods
and dairy alternatives
miso 4, 100
    Chicken Miso Soup 99–100
    Miso-glazed Halibut Steaks 134–5

molasses 11
mood enhancement 4
mooli: Chunky Kimchi 36–7
mould 9, 10, 12, 13, 17, 18, 22
    mould allergies 18
mushrooms: Thai-style Vegetable
    Omelette 103

nata de coco 149
natto 140
noodles
    Miso-glazed Halibut Steaks 134–5
    Noodles in Chilled Beef Broth 96–8
    Thai-style Vegetable Omelette 103
nuts
    Blueberry Brain Booster 159
    Coconut Kefir Cheesecake 146–7
    Creamy Kefir Carrot Cake 154–5
    see also almonds; pistachio nuts

obesity 7, 8
oranges
    Carrot Kraut with Ginger and Orange 41
    Fresh Fruit Jelly 144–5
    Mango and Orange Wake-up 158
    Sparkling Orange Juice 80
organic ingredients 8, 10–11, 19

pak choi 19
parsnips 19
pasta: Smoked Salmon and Pasta Salad with
    Avocado Kefir Dressing 111
pears 19
    Avocado, Coconut and Pear Smoothie 162
    Noodles in Chilled Beef Broth 96–8
peas
    Minted Pea and Broad Bean Soup with
        Yogurt 101
    Miso-glazed Halibut Steaks 134–5
    peppers 19
    Cauliflower, Carrot and Pepper Pickles 31
    Classic Kimchi 34–5
    Couscous and Grilled Pepper Salad with
        Labneh 118–19
    Mixed Vegetable Slaw 26–7
    Thai-style Vegetable Omelette 103

pH levels 17
phytic acid 4
pickle weights 13–14
pickling spices 21
Pineapple Pickle 44
pistachio nuts
   Pistachio and Almond Lassi 160
   Yogurt Cake with Lemon and
      Pistachios 156
plastic bowls and containers 12, 14
pork
   Hunter's Stew 128–9
   Paprika Pork 130–1
pouchitis 6
probiotics 3, 4, 8
processed foods 2

Quinoa Falafels in Wholemeal Pittas with Mixed Vegetable Slaw 122–4

radishes 19, 33
   Classic Kimchi 34–5
   Pickled Radishes with Red Onion and Apple 32–3
Rejuvelac 5, 77–8
   Pistachio and Almond Lassi 160
   Tropical Fruit Salad 149
rice
   Chicken Miso Soup 99–100
   glutinous rice 140
   Japanese Red Rice with Natto 139–40
   Minted Pea and Broad Bean Soup with Yogurt 101
   Salmon and Kimchi Sushi Rolls 114–15

sake 100
salads
   Couscous and Grilled Pepper Salad with Labneh 118–19
   Marinated Herring and Beetroot Salad 110
   Sesame Chicken Salad 120–1
   Smoked Salmon and Pasta Salad with Avocado Kefir Dressing 111
   Summer Chicken Caesar Salad 112–13
salt 9–10, 17, 22
   sea salt 9
   table salt 9
sauerkraut 13, 14, 19, 21
   Hunter's Stew 128–9
   Paprika Pork 130–1
   Simple Sauerkraut 23–4
   Spiced Red Cabbage and Apple Sauerkraut 25
scoby (Symbiotic Culture of Bacteria and Yeast) 73, 75–6
seasonings, spices and flavours 21–2
serotonin 2, 4
sieves 14
smoked salmon
   Salmon and Kimchi Sushi Rolls 114–15
   Smoked Salmon and Pasta Salad with Avocado Kefir Dressing 111
smoothies
   Avocado, Coconut and Pear Smoothie 162
   Blueberry Brain Booster 159
   Breakfast Blend 157
   Mango and Orange Wake-up 158
   Pistachio and Almond Lassi 160
   Summer Fruit Sipper 161
soups
   Borscht 102
   Chicken Miso Soup 99–100
   Minted Pea and Broad Bean Soup with Yogurt 101
   Noodles in Chilled Beef Broth 96–8
sourdough
   California Sourdough 88–9
   Easy Sourdough Starter 87
   Sourdough Loaf 84–6
   Sourdough Pancakes 141
Soured Cream 56
sourness 20
soya beans
   lecithin 160
   natto 140
   Smoked Salmon and Pasta Salad with Avocado Kefir Dressing 111
   tempeh 137
spoons 14
starter culture 19, 20–1
sterilising equipment 15–16, 17
stompers 14

strawberries: Summer Fruit Sipper 161
Sucanat 81
sugar 10–11
symbiosis 2

tahini
   Couscous and Grilled Pepper Salad with Labneh 118–19
   Creamy Hummus 107
tampers 14
tannin 22, 29
tea: Kombucha 73–6
tempeh 4, 137
   Tempeh Coconut Korma 136–7
   Tempeh Veggie-burgers 138
thermometer 15
tomatoes
   Creamy Seafood Wraps with Kimchi 125
   Fresh Tomato and Kefir Cheese Bruschetta 116–17
   Hunter's Stew 128–9
   Paprika Pork 130–1
   Probiotic Tomato Ketchup 43
turnips 19
   Pickled Beetroot and Turnips 40
   Tempeh Coconut Korma 136–7

ulcerative colitis 6

vegetable pounders 14
vegetables
   fermenting 19–22
   see also individual index entries
vegetarians and vegans 21, 100, 122, 137, 154
vinegar 22

water
   bottled 11
   filtered tap 11

watermelon: Summer Fruit Sipper 161
wheat berries 78
   Rejuvelac 5, 77–8
wheatgrass 78
whey 21
   Greek Yogurt and Whey 50
   Soured Cream 56
Worcestershire sauce 131

yeasts 1, 2, 4, 7, 17
   wild yeast 84
yogurt 3, 6, 8, 47
   Berry Frozen Yogurt 143
   Breakfast Blend 157
   Coconut Drinking Yogurt 54
   Coconut Yogurt 52–3
   flavourings 50
   Greek Yogurt and Whey 50
   Griddled Asparagus with Yogurt Hollandaise 104
   Labneh 51
   live yogurt 50
   Mediterranean Lamb Kebabs 132
   Minted Pea and Broad Bean Soup with Yogurt 101
   Pistachio and Almond Lassi 160
   Salad Dressing 113
   Smoked Aubergine and Yogurt Dip 106
   starter sachets 55
   Tempeh Coconut Korma 136–7
   Tzatziki 105
   Yogurt 49–50
   Yogurt Cake with Lemon and Pistachios 156
   'Yogurt Cream' 145
   Yogurt-spiced Chicken Skewers 108
   see also whey